The Doings of the

Fifteenth Infantry Brigade

August 1914 to March 1915

L. DE ST A.   J. T. W.   G.   A. L. M.-B.   R. E. B.

SOME OF BRIGADE HEADQUARTERS.

Photo by
Lieut. H. M. Gadell, R.E.

The Doings of the
Fifteenth Infantry Brigade

August 1914 to March 1915

BY

ITS COMMANDER

Brigadier-General COUNT GLEICHEN,
(now Major-General Lord Edward Gleichen),
K.C.V.O., C.B., C.M.G., D.S.O.

William Blackwood & Sons
Edinburgh and London
1917

NOTE.

THE following pages—not in the first in-
stance intended for publication—contain an
expanded version of the very scrappy Diary
which I kept in France from day to day.

The version was intended for private
home consumption only, and has necessarily
had to be pruned of certain personal matters
before being allowed to make its bow to
the public. I have purposely refrained from
adding to it in the light of subsequent
events.

I trust that the reader will consequently
bear in mind the essentially individual and
impressionist aspects of this little work,
and will not expect to find either rigidly
historical, professional, or critical matter
therein.

G.

14th August 1917.

CONTENTS.

SKETCH-MAPS.

ILLUSTRATION.

The Doings of the
Fifteenth Infantry Brigade.

August 1914 to March 1915.

IN accordance with the order received at
Belfast at 5.30 P.M. on the 4th, the 15th
Brigade started mobilizing on the 5th
August 1914, and by the 10th was complete
in all respects. We were practically ready
by the 9th, but a machine-gun or two and
some harness were a bit late arriving from
Dublin — not our fault. Everything had
already been rehearsed at mobilization in-
spections, held as usual in the early summer,
and all went like clock-work. On the 8th
we got our final orders to embark on the
14th, and on the 11th the embarkation
orders arrived in detail.

Brigade Headquarters consisted of myself,
Captain Weatherby (Oxford L.I.) as Brigade

A

Major, Captain Moulton - Barrett (Dorsets), Staff Captain, Captain Roe (Dorsets), Brigade Machine - Gun Officer, Lieutenant Cadell, R.E., Signalling Officer, and Lieutenant Beilby, Brigade Veterinary Officer. Military Police, A.S.C. drivers, postmen, and all sorts of odds and ends arrived from apparently nowhere in particular, and fitted together with extraordinary little effort. The battalions grew to unheard-of sizes, and by the time that all was complete the Brigade numbered 127 officers, 3958 men, 258 horses, and 74 vehicles.

Aug. 14th.

The Cheshires[1] and Bedfords[2] arrived by train in the early morning of the 14th from 'Derry and Mullingar and went straight on board their ships — Brigade Headquarters, Dorsets,[3] and half the Norfolks[4] being in one, Cheshires and the other half of the Norfolks in another, and the Bedfords in a third.

Great waving of handkerchiefs and cheer-

[1] 1st Batt. (Lieut.-Col. D. C. Boger).
[2] 1st Batt. (Lieut.-Col. C. R. Griffith, D.S.O.).
[3] 1st Batt. (Lieut.-Col. L. J. Bols, D.S.O.).
[4] 1st Batt. (Lieut.-Col. C. R. Ballard).

ing as we warped slowly out of Belfast
docks at 3 P.M. and moved slowly down the
channel.

Aug. 16th.

The weather was beautifully fine on the
passage, and on the 16th we all arrived at
our destination.

The Bedfords had arrived on the previous
tide to ourselves, and were already fast
alongside the quay. Orders were received
from the Disembarking Officer, and we dis-
embarked and formed up independently and
marched off to Rest Camp No. 8, six miles
off on the hills above Havre.

It had been pouring heavily on shore for
two days, though it was quite fine when we
landed; so the ground where we were to
encamp was mostly sopping. It was not
easy to find in the dark, especially as the
sketch-maps with which we were provided
most distinctly acted up to their names.
Added to these difficulties, a motor-lorry
had stuck on the way up and blocked our
transport for the night. I rode ahead alone,
but had immense difficulty in finding the
Brigade Headquarters Camp, which was
quite a long way from the other battalion

camps. These were dotted on the open
fields at some distance from each other,
and pitched in no particular order, so that
by the time I had got my bearings and
brought in the battalions, it was about
11 P.M. There was of course no baggage,
nor anything to sleep on except the bare
ground under the tents, with our saddles
for pillows; and as a pleasant excitement
nearly all our horses stampeded about 2 A.M.,
tore up their picketing-pegs from the soft
ground, and disappeared into the darkness
in different directions.

Aug. 17th.

Daylight, however, brought relief, and a
certain amount of our transport; and all the
horses were discovered in course of time
and brought back. Most of the morning
was spent, unsuccessfully, in trying to bring
up the remaining transport up a steep and
narrow road which was the only alternative
to the blocked one. But some of the horses
jibbed, and we had eventually to give it up
and bring up supplies by hand.

The battalions were comfortably settled
down under the expectation of another
night there; but at 2.15 P.M. we got orders
to move off by train at night. This we did

from three different stations, at times vary-
ing from 12 midnight to 5.45 A.M., having
arrived according to order at the stations
four hours previously. This is the French
system, allowing four hours for the entraining of a unit. Although a lot of man-
handling had to be done, and the trucks
were not what we had been accustomed to,
we all entrained in about forty minutes, so
had any amount of time to spare.

Silver (my first charger) was very bobbery
as usual, and it took a good half-hour to
persuade him to enter his truck. Once in,
he slept like a lamb.

Aug. 18th.

We were comfortable enough, though
packed like sardines, and with three-quarters
of an hour's rest at Rouen for coffee, and
another rest at Amiens—where we heard
that poor General Grierson, our Corps Commander, was dead—broke a blood-vessel
in the train — we arrived at Busigny at
2.15 P.M. Here we found Captain Hyslop[1]
(Dorsets), who had been sent ahead from
Belfast, and who gave us orders to detrain
at Le Cateau, a few miles farther on. I

---

[1] Hyslop was very severely wounded six days afterwards
and taken prisoner, but exchanged later on.

must say that all these disembarking and training arrangements were extraordinarily well done, and reflected great credit on the Allied staffs combined. No hitch, no fuss, no worry, everybody got their orders in time, and all necessary arrangements had been carefully thought out beforehand.

We arrived at Le Cateau at 3.10 P.M., and detrained in half an hour, baggage and all. The battalions marched off to their billets,—Dorsets and Headquarters to Ors, the other three battalions to Pommereuil: nice clean little villages both of them.

When about halfway out to Ors—I was riding on ahead of the Brigade with only Weatherby—we were met by a motor bikist with a cypher telegram for me. This stumped us completely, as, not yet having reported to the Division, we had not yet received the local field cypher-word; so, seeing a car approaching with some "brass hats" in it, I rode across the road and stopped it, with a view to getting the key. To my horror, Sir John French and Sir A. Murray descended from the car and demanded to know why I had stopped them. I explained and apologised, and they were very pleasant about it; but on looking at the wire they said that I could disregard it, as they knew what it was about, and it was of no particular importance by this time; so we pursued our way in peace.

The billeting had already been done for us by our (5th) Divisional Staff, and we found no difficulty in shaking down.

I was billeted on a small elderly lady of the name of Madame W——, who was kindness itself, and placed herself and her house at our disposal; but I regret to say that when our men, in search of firewood, picked up some old bits of plank lying about in the garden, she at first made a shocking fuss, tried to make out that it was a whole timber stack of new wood, and demanded fifty francs compensation. She eventually took two francs and was quite content.

Here it was that Saint André joined us, having been cast off by the 5th Divisional Staff at Landrecies as a superfluous interpreter. Looking like an ordinary French subaltern with a pince-nez, he was in fact a Protestant pastor from Tours, son of the Vicomte de Saint André, very intelligent and "cultured," with a great sense of humour and extremely keen. I really cannot speak too highly of him, for he was a most useful addition to the Staff. In billeting and requisitioning, and in all matters requiring tact in connection with the inhabitants or the French Army, he was invaluable. I used him later as A.D.C. in action, and as *Officier de liaison* with the French troops. I don't know what his knowledge of divinity may have been, but if it was anything like equal to his military knowledge it must have been considerable. He had studied theology at Edinburgh, and his English was very fluent, luckily untouched by a Scottish accent. He was always bubbling over with vitality and go, and plunged into English with the recklessness of his race; when he couldn't express himself clearly he invented words which were the joy of the Mess,—"pilliate," "whizzle," "contemporative," and dozens of others that I can't remember; and what used to charm us particularly was that he so often went out of his way to put the accent on the wrong syllable, such as in bilyétting, brígade, áttack, ambassádor, &c. He was, indeed, a great acquisition to the Brigade.[1]

---

[1] He was subsequently awarded the D.S.O. and Croix de Guerre (aux Palmes) for excellent and gallant work achieved under fire.

Aug. 19th.

Next morning I rode across to have a look at the other battalions. The transport horses of the Cheshires were perhaps not all they might have been, but it was the particular stamp of Derry horse that was at fault, and not the battalion arrangements. Otherwise we were ready for the fray.

Aug. 20th.

We had arrived on the Tuesday (18th), and on the Thursday Sir C. Fergusson (commanding 5th Division) paraded the Brigade by battalions and made them a short speech, telling us we were to move on the morrow, and giving us a few technical tips about the Germans and how to meet their various wiles, largely about machine-guns and their methods of attack in large numbers. The Bedfords were the most interested audience, and interrupted him every now and then with " 'Ear, 'ear,' and a little handclapping at important points. I think the General was a little nonplussed at this attention: I know I was. Whether it was due or not to the audience being accustomed to attending

political meetings at home, or to the air of
Bedfordshire being extremely vitalising I
don't know, but once or twice afterwards
when the battalion was addressed by General
Smith Dorrien,[1] and even by Sir J. French,
they showed their approbation in the
manner above set forth—somewhat to my
confusion.

Aug. 21st.

Next day we moved off early. I already
found myself overburdened with kit — although I had not even as much as the
regulation 150 lb.—and I left a camp-bed
and a thick waistcoat and various odds
and ends behind in Madame W——'s cupboard, under the firm belief that I might
at some future period send for it if I
wanted it. Alas! the Germans have now
been at Ors for close on three years.

A hot march of about fifteen miles brought
us to Gommignies. Stragglers, I regret to
say, were already many—all of them reservists, who had not carried a pack for
years. They had every intention of keeping up, of course, but simply could not.
I talked to several of them and urged

---

[1] Commanding of course the 2nd Corps (composed of the
3rd and 5th Divisions).

them along, but the answer was always the same—"Oh, I'll get along all right, sir, after a bit of rest; but I ain't accustomed to carrying a big weight like this on a hot day," and their scarlet streaming faces certainly bore out their views. To do them justice, they practically all did turn up. I was afraid that, in spite of great care and the numerous orders I had issued about the fitting and greasing of new boots, it was the boots which were at fault; but it was not so, except in a very few cases.

Our billeting parties had, of course, been sent ahead and started on their work. It was naturally quite new work to them, and it took a lot of time at first—two and three hours—before the men were settled. Nowadays it takes half an hour, or at most an hour, as everybody knows his job, and also takes what is given him at once, squash or no squash. After a little campaigning men very quickly find out that it is better to shake down at once, even in uncomfortable billets, than to hang about and try to get better ones. Here we got first touch, though very indirectly, with the enemy, in the shape of a French patrol of *Chasseurs à Cheval* (in extraordinarily *voyant* light-blue tunics and shakos), who had come in from somewhere north after having seen some "Uhlans" and hunted them off. I sent the news, such as it was, on to the Division.

And here I must lay stress on the fact that throughout the campaign we did not know in the least what was happening elsewhere. Beyond the fact that the 3rd Division was somewhere on our right, and that the French cavalry was believed to be covering our left front, we did not know at this period what the movement was about or where the Germans were supposed to be. We trusted to our superiors to do what was necessary, and plunged blindly into the "fog of war."

The usual proceedings on the ordinary line of march were that, on receiving "Divisional Orders," which arrived at any time in the afternoon, or often at night, we compiled "Brigade Orders" on them. Divisional Orders give one first of all any information about the enemy which it is advisable to impart, then the intention of the Divisional General—whether he means to fight on the morrow, or march, or stay where he is, &c., &c.; and if he means to

march he gives the direction in which the
Division is to proceed, the order of march,
by brigades, artillery, divisional troops such
as R.E., heavy batteries, divisional cavalry,
&c., &c., and generally says where and
how the transport is to march, whether
with its own troops or some way behind,
and if so, where; and gives directions as
to the supplies, where the refilling-point,
rendezvous for supply carts, and railhead
are, and many other odds and ends, especially as to which brigade is to provide
the advanced- or rear-guard, who is to
command it, at what time the head of the
column and the heads of all the formations are to pass a given point, and so on.
On receiving these orders we have to make
out and issue similarly composed Brigade
Orders in detail, giving the order of march
of the battalions and Brigade Headquarters,
how much rations are to be carried on the
men and in the cook-waggons, what is to
happen to the supply and baggage waggons,
whether B transport (vehicles not absolutely
necessary in the fighting line) are to be
with the A transport in rear of their respective battalions, or to be bunched up
by themselves behind the Brigade, with

similar detailed orders about the advanced-
guard or rear-guard, and the time to a
minute as to when each detail is to pass
a given point, the position of the Brigadier
in the column, the point to which reports
are to be sent, &c., &c. These orders might
be written in anything from fifteen to fifty
minutes according to the movement required, and then had to be quadruplicated
and sent out to the battalions by their
respective orderlies, or by wire. By the
time the battalions had written out and
transmitted their own orders to their companies it was sometimes very late indeed;
but as the campaign went on, orders got
more and more simplified somehow, and
things got done quicker than at the beginning of the *premier pas.*

The country through which we were
passing was that technically described by
novelists as "smiling." That is to say, it
was pretty, in a mild sort of way, clean,
green, with tidy farmhouses and cottages,
and fields about ripe for the harvest. Plenty
of orchards there were too, with lots of
fruit - trees alongside the roads, and the
people were most kind in offering us fruit
and milk and water and coffee and even

wine as we went along. But this could not be allowed on the march, as it would have led to men falling out without permission, and also to drinking more than was good for them whilst marching. Except, therefore, occasionally, and then only during the ten minutes' halt that we had in each hour, I did not allow these luxuries to be accepted.

Gommignies was a nice shady little town, and the Notaire gave me an excellent bed-room in his big house; whilst I remember that I made acquaintance there with the excellent penny cigar of the country.

Aug. 22nd.

Off at cock-crow next day, the country got uglier, blacker, more industrial, and more thickly populated as we pushed on through the heat, and by the time we crossed the Belgian frontier we felt indeed that we were in another land.

The beastly paved road with cobbles, just broad enough for one vehicle and extremely painful to the feet, whilst the remainder of the road on both sides was deep in dust or caked mud, was a most offensive feature; the people staring and crowding round the troops were quite a different type from the courteous French peasants; and whilst in France not a single able-bodied civilian had been visible—all having joined the Army— in Belgium the streets were crowded with men who, we felt most strongly, ought to have been fighting in the ranks.

There was a great block in Dour, which we reached after a fourteen-mile march, and in spite of all attempts at keeping the streets clear it was some time before we could get through. Part of the Division was halting there for the night, and the municipal authorities were extremely slow in allotting billets and keeping their civilian waggons in order.

From Dour onwards it was a big straggling sort of suburban town—tramways down the side, dirty little houses lining the street, great chimneys belching (I believe that is the correct term) volumes of black smoke, huge mountains of slag in all directions, rusty brickfields littered with empty tins, old paper, and bits of iron, and other similarly unlovely views. The only thing to be said in favour of this industrial scrap- heap was that the smoke was not quite so sooty as it looked, and things one touched did not "come off" quite so black as might have been expected. Otherwise there was no attraction.

Half a mile on or more was Bois de Boussu, and here we were halted to allow of a cavalry brigade moving down the street. We waited some time, and eventually it arrived, not coming down the street but across it from east to west. I am ashamed to say that I have forgotten which it was, but the 4th Dragoon Guards, I think, were in it. They crossed at a trot, men and horses both looking very fit and workmanlike, and disappeared westwards through the haze of the factories; any more impossible country for cavalry — except perhaps the London Docks—I have never seen.

We shortly afterwards got orders to billet in Bois de Boussu and Dour, the real Boussu being another half mile on. But where the whole countryside was one vast straggling town, it was impossible to say where one town ended and the other began. Even the inhabitants didn't know.

Moulton - Barrett and Saint André had already got to work on the billeting, and the Norfolks and Cheshires were shortly accommodated in some factories up the road, whilst the Bedfords and Dorsets were

B

moved back nearly into Dour, into a brewery and some mine-offices respectively, if I remember rightly. Brigade Headquarters was installed in an ultra-modern Belgian house and garden belonging to one M. Durez, a very civil little man, head of some local mining concern. There was a Madame Durez too, plump and good-natured, and a girl and a boy, and they were profuse in their hospitality. The only drawback about the meals, excellent as they were, was the appalling length of time occupied in their preparation and consumption; it was almost impossible to get away from them, even though there was so much to do.

So much was there to be done that I feel now as though we had been there a week, or at least three days; but on looking at my diary I find we arrived there at midday on Saturday the 22nd, and left at midnight on Sunday the 23rd.

On the Saturday afternoon there were rumours of the Germans being on the other side of the Mons-Condé Canal, not far off. The 13th and 14th Brigades were in front of us, strung out and holding the Canal line, ourselves being in Divisional Reserve. Where the exact left of the 5th Division was I cannot remember at this moment, but I am sure that it was not farther west than Pommeroeul bridge, with, I believe, French or English cavalry on its left.

Saturday afternoon was spent in studying the ground in our front and looking to the approaches and the arrangements for the Brigade. Our front was of course well covered, but there were numerous little matters to be seen to and a certain amount of confabulation with the Divisional Staff, which lived in the midst of a perpetual *va-et-vient* at the railway station at Dour. Our horses were picketed out in M. Durez's garden and the grubby little fields close by, and the Signal section and all the vehicles were stowed away there as best could be arranged; but all was enclosed, cramped, and unhandy, and the difficulty was to get a clear space anywhere. I walked with M. Durez in the evening to a tiny mound in his garden, from which he assured me a good view could be got; but although the sunset and colouring through the haze was rather picturesque, one couldn't see much. Durez was very apprehensive about his family and himself, and was most urgent in his inquiries as to what was going to happen. I could not tell him much beyond the rumour that the German force in front was reported not to be very big, and I advised him to stick it out as long as he could; but he was restless, with good reason as it turned out, and settled next day to take himself and his family away whilst there was yet time.

Aug. 23rd.

Next morning I got orders to go with Lieut.-Col. Tulloch, the Divisional Commanding Royal Engineer, to select a defensive position and entrench it. We got into a car, and went buzzing about in front of Boussu and round to the right as far as Wasmes; but I never saw such a hopeless place. There was no field of fire anywhere except to the left, just where the railway crossed the Boussu road, where, strange to say, the country opened out on to a "glacis-like" slope of stubble. Going was bad, up broken little roads over ground composed of a bewildering variety of slag-heaps 40 to 150 feet high, intersected with railway lines, mine heads, chimneys, industrial buildings, furnaces, and *usines* of all sorts, and thickening into suburbs consisting of narrow wind-

ing little streets and grubby little work-
men's houses. Here and there were open
spaces and even green fields, but nowhere
could a continuous field of fire be obtained.
The only thing was to select various *points
d'appui* with some sort of command, and
try and connect them up by patches of
entrenchments; but even this was very
difficult, as the line was so long and broken
that no unity of command was possible, and
the different patches were so separated and
so uneven, some having to be in front of
the general line and some in rear, that
they often could not flank or even see each
other.

At about midday several cyclists came
riding back in a great hurry from the
Canal, saying they had been attacked by a
big force of cavalry and been badly cut up;
that they had lost all their officers and
20 or 30 men killed, and the rest taken
prisoners. This was hardly a good beginning, but it eventually turned out that the
grand total losses were 1 officer (Corah of
the Bedfords) slightly wounded, 2 men
killed, and 3 missing.

Shortly after this the first German gun
was heard—at 12.40 P.M. I timed it—and

for the rest of the afternoon there was intermittent bombardment and numerous shell-bursts in the direction of the Canal, some of it our own Horse Artillery, but mostly German.

When we had roughly settled on our line, I shouted to a crowd of curious natives who had come out to watch us, and did not seem particularly friendly—as they were not at all sure that we were not Germans—to get all their friends together with pickaxes and shovels and start digging entrenchments where we showed them. It was Sunday afternoon, and all the miners were loafing about with nothing to do. The idea rapidly caught on, and soon they were hurrying off home for their tools, whilst we got hold of the best-dressed and most authoritative-looking men and showed them what we wanted done. It was scratch work, in more senses than one, as we had no time to lose and could not superintend, but had to tear from one point to another, raising men and showing them where the lines were to go, how deep the trenches were to be made, which way the earth was to be thrown, and all the rest of it.

On our way round we came also upon some

batteries of field artillery, disconsolately wending their way through the narrow streets, and with their reconnoitring officers out in all directions looking for positions; but they found none, and the Artillery did but little in the way of shooting that night. With their present experience I expect they would have done a good deal more.

Then we tore back, and I got the battalions out, or rather two companies of each battalion, set them to work, and sent out their other two companies to support them. The Norfolks were on the left, at the station, and eastwards down the line. Then came the Cheshires, a bit thrown back, in beastly enclosed country for the most part. One of the big slag-heaps had seemed to offer a good command, but to our disgust it was so hot that we could hardly stand on it, so that had to be given up. Other heaps again seemed to give a good position, and they were fairly cool; but when we scrambled up there was always something wrong— either there were more slag-heaps in front which blocked the view, or the heap ran to a point and there was not room for more than two men, or the slag-ridge faced the wrong way—it was a nightmare of a place.

Beyond the Cheshires came the Dorsets and Bedfords, pretty well together, and occupying some trenches on a high railway embankment, &c., but the position was not really satisfactory, and if attacked in force at night it would be very difficult to see or guard against the approach of the enemy. Nor, as I heard afterwards, had the inhabitants dug the trenches anything like deep enough, so that they formed but poor protection against the rain of shells that began to pour on them at nightfall.

All pointed to an attack by the enemy during the night or next day, but even then we had not the smallest idea of the enormous forces arrayed against us. We were told at first that there was perhaps a corps in front of us, but as a matter of fact there were three, if not four corps.

Having distributed the battalions as ordered—I had no Brigade Reserve in hand, having to cover such a broad front (nearly three miles, when my normal front, according to the text-books, should have been about 1000 yards) — myself and Brigade Headquarters were left rather "by our lone." M. and Madame Durez were packing up hard all, and disappeared with their

friends and family before dinner in a big
motor-car, making in the direction of Bavai
St Waast, to the south, where they had
friends; as, however, we retired through
there next day I don't expect they stayed
long, but continued their journey into
France. I don't know what became of
them. They had been most hospitable,
and placed the house and everything in it,
even a final dinner, at our disposal; but the
poor people were, of course, in a great state
of perturbation, and there was not much
except the house itself that we could make
use of.

As we were finishing dinner further orders
arrived from the Division. Weatherby and
I cantered down to the Divisional Staff to
learn details, and we got them shortly, to
the effect that the Cheshires and Norfolks
were to be left under direct command of the
Divisional Commander, whilst Brigade Headquarters was to be at Pâturages by sunrise
on the morrow, and to hold that with our
other two battalions on the right.

We "fell in" the Brigade Headquarters
about midnight and, after some trouble in
securing guides, moved off through a laby-
rinth of streets in the warm dark. Our

guides were local men, and we did not take
long to get to Warquignies, in the main
street of which we met the Headquarters of
the 13th Brigade, minus their Brigadier.
Here also were the K.O.S.B.'s in bivouac,
acting as Brigade Reserve to their (13th)
Brigade. The night was peaceful, and we
pushed on after a short rest, getting at
dawn to a steep hill which led down into
Pâturages.

Aug. 24th.

The latter was a fine big town with paved
streets and prosperous-looking houses, very
different from the grubby streets of Boussu ;
but I was troubled about the hill street, as
it was very steep and bad and narrow. How
we should get the transport up it again in
a hurry if it had to retire I did not know,
and two eminently respectable inhabitants
assured me that there was no other way
back unless I went right up to Wasmes—
from which direction firing was already
beginning — and returned *viâ* the north.
That didn't look healthy for the transport,
so I left most of the Brigade transport at
the top of the hill and only brought down
the Signal section.

At the entrance into Pâturages we found Currie, Cuthbert's (13th Brigade) Brigade Major, but Cuthbert was not there, so it was a little difficult to combine any action. However, we learnt that the other three battalions of the 13th Brigade were distributed in front of us on the north, and I received a message that the Dorsets and Bedfords had been obliged to fall back during the night and were holding the railway station at Wasmes and a bit east of that. The 13th Brigade had been along the line of the Canal the previous day and had been driven back by superior numbers, but had blown up some of the bridges. I heard afterwards that young Pottinger, a subaltern of the 17th Co. R.E., had been entrusted with blowing up one bridge, and that the charge had failed to explode. Whereupon he advanced under heavy fire close to the charge and had gallantly fired his revolver at it, which of course, as he knew, would have blown him sky-high with the bridge had he hit it. But either he missed the shot altogether or he hit the wrong part, and the thing didn't explode. And then he found himself cut off by Germans who had crossed elsewhere, and he had to leg it. So, unfortunately, that bridge was left intact.

I trotted ahead alone to try and find the Dorsets or the Bedfords, leaving Weatherby with other instructions. It was a long way to the station (Pâturages by name, but

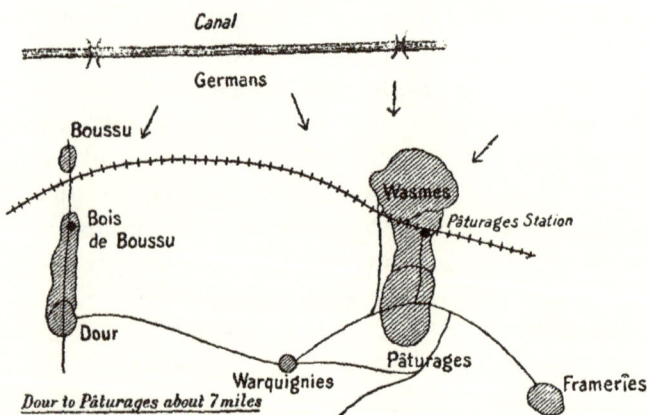

really in Wasmes), but I eventually found Griffith (O.C. Bedfords) and most of his men thereabouts. The Germans had apparently got round to the east, but we were holding them. The Dorsets were a bit further to the south-east, and I found them after a good many wrong turnings; and then there was little to do but pick up connection with whoever I could. By this time my staff had come up, and Weatherby and I cantered off to find General Haking, who, I understood, had brought up his 5th Brigade from the 2nd Division (1st Corps), and was somewhere towards Frameries. Him we found after some trouble, with only one battalion in action in fairly open country. It appeared that a message had been sent the night before from the 3rd Division that the Germans were threatening Pâturages and going to attack in force, and help was most urgently required; so General Haig had despatched Haking in a great hurry. The 5th Brigade made a forced march and arrived at Pâturages at 2 A.M., perspiring profusely. Not a sound. Fearing an ambush, they walked delicately, with scouts well out in front and to both flanks. Not a sign either of the British or the Germans,—empty streets, no one about, all quiet as death. So they bivouacked in the streets and were now thinking of falling back on their own corps, as there were only a few Germans in front of them and these wouldn't advance.

Where the 3rd Division exactly were I

could not at first find out, though I tried;
but I knew that they were holding the
country in the direction of Mons. Anyway, except for a good many shells flying
about, there was very little of the enemy
to see or hear, and Pâturages was safe at
all events for the present.

The Dorsets and Bedfords, however, had
had a pretty bad time on the previous
evening, and had lost a number of men,
though they had given the Germans a
good deal more than they got. The German shelling had been fairly accurate, and
their infantry had pushed on between the
slag-heaps and got their machine-guns to
work under cover in a horribly efficient
manner. Eventually our battalions had to
evacuate their trenches as their right flank
was being turned, and they fell back on
Wasmes and Pâturages, leaving most of
their packs behind them in the trenches.
They had taken them off to dig, and, being
hot, had fought without them, and then
this sudden outflanking movement had
necessitated a rapid falling back, so their
packs and most of their shovels had been
left behind. This was awkward, more especially hereafter, as, although the loss of

the greatcoat did not matter much in this hot weather, and certainly added to their marching power, still, the loss of the pack meant loss of spare socks and spare shirt—besides other things.

We snatched a little breakfast and coffee at an inn where the *patronne* was still in possession, and then things began to get more lively. Shells began to knock corners off the houses close by, and reports kept coming in that the enemy appeared to be advancing, though the bulk of his infantry was still some way off to the east. The Dorsets were rearranging their line so as not to be cut off, and I was standing with Bols (commanding Dorsets) and a few of his officers by the *estaminet* when a shrapnel burst with a tremendous crack close over our heads, bringing down branches and leaves in showers. Yet not a man or a horse was hit. The shrapnel bullets whizzed along the pavement in all directions, right among our feet, like hail it seemed; yet the only result was a lot of bad language from Saunders, who had got a nasty jar on the heel from one of the bullets: but it did not even cut the leather.

It now became time to get the Dorset

transport away, as things were getting
rather hot, and the crackling of rifles was
getting distinctly nearer. I thought of that
horrible hill and I looked at my map.
Yes — there certainly was a way round
back by the south-east, viâ the road along
which Weatherby and I had just come
back from interviewing Haking. So I
directed the transport to move that way
—there was a road branching off to the
right only 400 yards on and quite safe, as
I thought, for the firing was up north and
north-east, and this road lay south-south-
east.

Roe covered the withdrawal with his
company and was very anxious to lay an
ambush for the enemy. But they did not
seem inclined to oblige him, but kept head-
ing off in a more southerly direction. There
was no sign from the 3rd Division who, I
knew, were on our right; so, as my scouts
could not find them, I could only come to
the conclusion that the enemy had got in
between us, and if we didn't clear out soon
we should be in a bad way.

Suddenly there was a crackle of rifles
down the road along which the Dorset
transport had gone, and then nearly the

whole of the transport came galloping back,
a dead horse being dragged along in the
shafts of one of the waggons. Margetts,
the transport officer, rode past, revolver in
hand, and streaming with blood from the
shoulder, and one or two of the men and
horses had obviously been hit. What had
happened was that a few Germans had
penetrated on to the road where Weatherby
and I had passed in perfect safety only
a short time before and ambushed the
transport.

Margetts had very gallantly ridden direct
at the ambush with his revolver, shot down
one or two and bewildered the rest, and
thus given time for the transport to turn
round on the (luckily) broad road and
gallop back. The Pioneer Sergeant of the
Dorsets was killed, and so was a Brigade
Policeman who happened to be with the
transport. Otherwise almost the only loss
was an ammunition-cart with two horses
killed, and some damage was done to a pole
and wheel or two of the other vehicles.
Poor Nicholson (my servant), who should,
strictly speaking, have remained with the
Brigade transport and not come up at all,
had attached himself to the Dorset trans-

port without orders — wishing, I suppose,
to be handy in case he was required—and
had been shot down with the two or
three others. I believe he was killed; anyway, I never saw him again, poor fellow.
Margetts was nearly falling off his horse
with pain, so he dismounted and was
bandaged by the Medical Officer. But by
that time the transport vehicles had disappeared, and as he was fainting and was
not in a fit state to be carried, he had to be
left in the house of a Belgian doctor and
was taken prisoner shortly afterwards. We
heard of him later, and I am glad to say
his gallant action gained him a D.S.O.

Bols strung out half a company to defend
the place where we thought the Germans
would appear, but after waiting for ten
minutes we found we were practically "in
the air," as large forces of the enemy were
reported coming round our right flank, and
the firing on our left front got more and
more to the left, thus proving that the
Bedfords had been pushed back and were
retiring *via* Wasmes—as they had been told
to do if overwhelmed. Weatherby, who
had cantered off to get touch with them,
confirmed this; and as it was getting ex-

tremely "hot" (shells) where we were, I
gave the order to withdraw—only just in
time as it turned out.

The Dorsets formed a proper rear-guard
and held off the enemy, who were by this
time trickling in large numbers into the
town; but by good luck the Germans seemed
to funk coming on in formation, and by the
time we had got back to the foot of the steep
hill they didn't bother us any more except by
occasional shells. To my extreme annoyance
(in one way) we found another track leading round the hill, towards Warquignies, not
marked on the map; so those two wretched
inhabitants had told us quite wrong, and we
could have retired the transport this way
after all. Of course we took advantage of
it, and fell back slowly *viâ* Warquignies on
Blangies, where we arrived, with very few
casualties, about two.

Here we got orders at first to bivouac
for the night, but hardly had the men had
time to cook a meal and eat it than we
were ordered to continue the retirement
on Bavai St Waast, *viâ* Athis. As we got
on to the main road here we found a large
column of our own troops moving down
it, and there were German mounted patrols

at a respectful distance on both sides. We
fired at them occasionally, and they disappeared and then turned up again in twos
and threes on the skyline, evidently keeping touch with us.

Just beyond Athis we found the Norfolks, who had been fighting at Élouges all
the morning, and then we came across the
sad little remainder of the Cheshires —
only about 200 left out of 891 who had
gone into action that morning near Élouges.
It was horrible to hear of this appalling
loss. Shore was the only captain left, and
he was in command, with two or three
subalterns only. His story was that his
company had been in reserve to the other
three and had gone to occupy a farmhouse as told, that he had seen the three
companies extending to his right, and then
lost touch with them as they advanced
rapidly over the brow of the low rolling
ground. There was very heavy firing all
along the line, and eventually a staff officer
told him to fall back to his right rear and
rejoin his battalion. This he tried to do,
but he only came across a few wounded
and stragglers of his regiment, who told
him that the three companies had lost very

heavily, including Boger (commanding) and all their officers, and that there was practically nobody left. Shore did his best to find out and help, but a general retirement took place, and he and his men were swept back with the rest. Tahourdin, Stapylton, Dyer, Dugmore, and lots of others were reported killed, and poor Shore was in a terrible state of mind. (It turned out afterwards that all these officers were alive and prisoners, with a great number of their men, but at the time I could not find out exactly how it happened that the battalion got so cut up and lost such a desperate number.)

The Norfolks had lost poor Cresswell, their Adjutant — such a good fellow — and one or two other officers. But although their losses had been serious they were nothing like so bad as the Cheshires. It appears that our left about Élouges and to the west rear of Dour was heavily attacked by the enemy; that we were on the defensive with the 14th Brigade (Rolt), and these two battalions of the 15th, and the 2nd Cavalry Brigade (De Lisle); and that Sir C. F. called on the Cavalry to assist at a certain moment. De Lisle thereupon very

gallantly charged the German guns, but he
started from some distance off, and not
only were the horses blown before they
got there, but there was a lot of wire
between them and the Germans which
they couldn't get through. So, after
losing heavily, they wheeled to the right
to get out of the way. What happened
in detail to the 14th Brigade I frankly
don't know, but I fear the guns of the 5th
Division lost pretty heavily at this period.

Two companies of the Bedfords had joined
us by this time, but I was rather nervous
about the rest, including Griffith, for I had
had no word of him since Pâturages. However, as we passed through Houdain he
turned up from a side road with the rest
of his battalion, having had a pretty rough
time in getting out of Wasmes.

By dusk we had got on to the open
country near St Waast, and here we
found that the Division was bivouacking.
Although it was nearly dark, and the
Brigade had been scattered, with its transport, over a lot of country during the day,
it all came together again, including its
empty supply waggons, in a marvellous
way, and managed to find its way through

all the other troops in the dark to its rightful bivouac space—some fields covered with standing crops. Water was of course the difficulty, but some was discovered in the shape of a small stream half a mile off, over hedges and ditches; and after the Norfolks had been put out on outpost to cover our rear, and we had had some food, we slept the sleep of the dog-tired.

I remember Cadell came out as cook that evening, for he fried a lugubrious mess of biscuits, jam, and sardines together in a mess-tin, and insisted on all of us having some. Up to this point our messing had not been entirely happy, for an old soldier whom I had taken on in Belfast, on his own statement that he had been second cook in his officers' mess, turned out an absolute fraud. He could hardly even poach an egg, and hadn't the smallest idea of cooking. I am sure he had never been inside an officers' mess either, for when he was deposed from the office of cook to that of mess waiter, he knew nothing about that either, and could not even wash up. Private Brown, who was supposed at first only to cook for the men of the Brigade Headquarters, was therefore elevated to the

proud status of Officers' cook, and made a
thundering good one (till he was wounded
at Ypres); and the Belfast man was given
the sack at the earliest opportunity and
sent home,—only to appear later in the
field as a corporal of the Irish Rifles!

Aug. 25th.

Next morning the Brigade was on the
move before daylight, and was told off as
part of the main body of the Division, the
14th Brigade forming the rear-guard. We
had not had much to eat the night before,
or in fact the whole day, and as the rations
had not come up during the night, the men
had devilish little breakfast—nor we either.

We were told to requisition what we
could from the country, but though St
André and myself did our best, and rode
on ahead of the Brigade, routing out the
dwellers of the farmhouses and buying
chickens and cheese and oats wherever possible, there was very little to be had.

There were already a great many inhabitants on the road fleeing south-westwards,
pitiful crowds of women and old men and
children, carrying bundles on their backs, or
wheeling babies and more bundles in wheel-

barrows, or perambulators, or broken-down carts. Some of the peasant women were wearing their best Sunday gowns of black bombazine and looked very hot and uncomfortable; children with their dolls or pet dogs, old women and men hobbling along, already very tired though the sun had not been up more than an hour or two, and sturdy young mothers carrying an extraordinary quantity of household stuff, trooped along, all of them anxiously asking how far off the Germans were, and whether we could hold them off, or whether they would all be killed by them, — it was a piteous sight. We warned all the people who were still in their cottages to stay there and not to run away, as their houses would only be pillaged if they were not there, but I fear that few took our advice.

It seemed a very long march that day, down the perfectly straight road skirting the Mormal forest and on to Le Cateau. It was, as a matter of fact, only a little over twenty miles, but the hot day, with very little food, was most trying for the men. We had one good rest at Englefontaine, where we bought a lot of food— bread and cheese, and apples and plums,

and a little meat — but it was not much.
The rest of the road was bare and hot,
leading over down - like country past the
town of Le Cateau, and on to the heights
to the west of it. Many aeroplanes, British,
French, and German, were skimming about,
and numerous bodies of French cavalry
could be seen moving about the downs and
the roads in the rear.

We had received orders on the road to
occupy part of an entrenched position to
the west of Le Cateau, and Weatherby and
I rode ahead to look at it and apportion
it off as the battalions came up.   The
trenches, we considered, were quite well
sited. They were about 3 feet deep, and
had been dug by the inhabitants under, I
think, French supervision; but, judging by
our subsequent experience, they were nothing
like deep enough and placed on much too
exposed ground; and the artillery pits were
far too close up—though correct according
to the then text-books.

I put a few men into the trenches as an
observing line, and sent the commanding
officers round to study them in case we
had to hold them in force on the morrow,
and bivouacked the rest of the Brigade

half a mile behind them. Although we seemed to have done a good day's work already, it was then only about 3 P.M., for we had started about 3.30 A.M. We got a good deal more food—bully beef and bis- cuits—here, besides a cart-load of very smelly cheeses and some hams and vege- tables and fresh bread, and the men got their stomachs fairly full by sundown.

The 13th Brigade came in a bit later and formed up on our right, but the 14th Brigade, who had been doing rear-guard, did not get in till nightfall, and were much exhausted.

The enemy, however, bar cavalry, had not pressed on in any strength, and we were left fairly well alone during the night.

It began to rain heavily in the evening, and we had a wet dinner in the open. There were various disturbances in the night, especially when some men in the trenches began firing at some probably imaginary Germans; but otherwise all ranks got a fair amount of sleep.

Aug. 26th.
The orders overnight were that we were to continue the retirement first thing in

the morning; but when morning came the Germans were so close that it was decided that it would be impossible to do so, and fresh orders were issued to hold the position we were in.

Accordingly we took up our positions as we had settled overnight, and started all necessary preparations—deepening trenches, arranging telephone wires and communications, and putting the village of Troisvilles, on our left, in a state of defence.

The Dorsets were to hold this village and several hundred yards of trenches to the east of it. On their right came the Bedfords in trenches, with of course a proportion in support, and the Cheshires were put in a dip of the ground in rear of them. The 13th Brigade was on the right of the Bedfords, with the K.O.S.B.'s touching them. The Norfolks I put in a second line, in rear of the right of the Bedfords and the left of the K.O.S.B.'s, mostly along a sunken road where they dug themselves well into the banks. The 27th Brigade of Artillery, under Onslow, was put under my orders; two batteries of it were in our right rear, and the third was taken away by Sir C. F., to strengthen the right I believe. A battery of the 15th Artillery Brigade was also put in close behind the Bedfords, in the dip of ground afore-mentioned, whence they did excellent execution without being seen by the enemy. Divisional Headquarters were at Reumont, a mile behind us, with a wood in between; but we were, of course, connected up by telephone with them, as well as with our battalions and our artillery. We—*i.e.*, the Brigade Headquarters—sat in the continuation of the hollow sandy road, in rear of the Bedfords and on the left of the Norfolks.

The morning was distinctly cool after the rain, and I remember that I wore my woolly till about 11 o'clock. Our horses were stowed away a few hundred yards to our left, in a hollow; and the extraordinary thing was that neither they nor ourselves got shelled as long as we were there, though some shrapnel burst occasionally only a hundred yards off or so in different directions.

We were in position by 7 o'clock, as far as I can remember; but unless one keeps a record the whole time one is very liable to err—and I won't swear that it was not 8 o'clock. Some shells began to arrive about then, but did no harm. On our left was the

9th Brigade (3rd Division), and the shelling began to develop pretty heavily in their direction. Our guns were of course in action by this time, and for the first two or three hours the air was full of shells and very little Infantry fire was heard. The 4th Division had arrived only that morning, I believe by train, and was guarding the left flank of the line, assisted by our Cavalry. Behind the town of Le Cateau, on the extreme right, was the 19th Brigade. Then came the 14th Brigade, then the 13th, then ourselves, and then the 3rd Division; so we were about the right centre.

The Dorsets were hard at work putting Troisvilles into a strong state of defence, and were helped by some of our Divisional Sappers, I believe the 59th Co. R.E. (but it might have been the 17th).

There was a local French ambulance— civilian I think—in Troisvilles, and several of our own R.A.M.C. personnel there; but the Divisional ambulances were farther to the rear, and as the wounded began to come in from the right front we sent them back towards Reumont. St André was very useful in galloping backwards and forwards between Troisvilles and Brigade Headquarters

—I kept him for that, as I wanted my proper staff for other staff work; but all of them paid a visit or two there once or twice. The enemy's shells were now falling fast on our left about Inchy, but seemed to do extraordinarily little damage there; and during the first hours it was really more of a spectacular piece for us than a battle. However, we were of course kept busy sending and receiving wires from all parts, and every now and then a few wounded came in from our front. We were also bucked up by hearing that a French Cavalry Division was coming to help us from Cambrai; but I don't know whether it ever materialised.

As the day wore on, the Bedfords got engaged with infantry in their front, but neither they nor the Dorsets got anything very much to shoot at; and though a German machine-gun or two pushed pluckily forward and did a certain amount of damage from hidden folds in the ground, I think we accounted for them—anyway we stopped their shooting after a short time.

Meanwhile the 13th Brigade and the guns on our right were catching it very hot. There seemed an enormous number of guns against us (I believe, as a matter

of fact, there were nearer 700 than 600),
and our batteries were suffering very
heavily. So were the 14th and 19th
Brigades—the latter being a scratch one
composed of units from the lines of communication under Laurence Drummond.

At one moment—it must have been about
12 o'clock or later—I saw to my horror the
best part of a company of Bedfords leave
their trenches in our front and retire slowly
and in excellent order across the open. So
I got on my horse and galloped out to see
what they were doing and to send them
back, as it seemed to me that some of the
K.O.S.B.'s were falling back too, in sym-
pathy. I'm afraid that my language was
strong; but I made the Bedfords turn about
again, although their officer explained that
he was only withdrawing, by superior battalion orders, in order to take up an advanced position further on the right; and
with some of the Cheshires, whom I picked
up on the way, they advanced again in
extended order.

They got back again to their trenches
without any casualties to speak of, and I
was much gratified by a message I received
shortly afterwards from my right (I think

Cuthbert or the gunners) thanking me warmly for my most valuable counter-attack, which had considerably relieved the pressure in their front !

On our immediate right the Norfolks were occupied for several hours in trying to cut down a very big tree, which was about the most conspicuous feature in the whole of our position, and formed an excellent object on which the enemy could range. It was all very well; but as soon as they had cut it half through, so as to fall to the south, the south wind, which was blowing pretty strongly, not only kept it upright but threatened to throw it over to the north. This would have been a real disaster, as it would have blocked completely the sunken road along which the ammunition carts, to say nothing of artillery and other waggons, would have had to come. So it had to be guyed up with ropes, with much difficulty; and even when teams hung on and hauled on the ropes, they could make little impression — the wind was so strong. Eventually they did manage to get it down, but even so it formed a fairly conspicuous mark. (It was so big that it was marked on the map.)

D

Inchy was now the centre of an appalling bombardment. A crowd of Germans had got into it, it appeared, and the village was being heavily shelled by both sides—British and German. Several houses and haystacks caught fire, and the poor devils inside must have had a terrible time. The 3rd Division was holding its own, but was being heavily attacked by the enemy's infantry. However, we eventually got the better of it, and the 9th and 10th Brigades drove the Germans away from their trenches and pursued them some distance, much assisted by the fire of the Dorsets and the advance of one or two of their companies.

Things went on hammer-and-tongs for another hour or two; more and more wounded began coming in from the 13th Brigade, including a lot of K.O.S.B.'s. We turned Beilby, our veterinary officer, on to "first aid" for many of them and sent them on; but some of the shrapnel wounds were appalling. One man I remember lying across a pony; I literally took him for a Frenchman, for his trousers were drenched red with blood, and not a patch of khaki showing. Another man had the whole of the back of his thigh torn away; yet, after being bandaged, he hobbled gaily off, smoking a pipe. What struck me as curious was the large number of men hit in the face or below the knee,—there seemed few body wounds in comparison; but that may of course have been because those badly hit in the body were killed or unmovable. But one would see men apparently at their last gasp, with gruesome wounds on them and no more stretchers available, and yet five minutes afterwards they had disappeared.

Time was getting on, and the thunder and rain of German shells seemed unceasing; they appeared to come now not only from all along the front and the right front, but from our right as well, and our guns were replying less and less. Reports began to come in from the right of batteries wiped out (the 28th R.F.A. Brigade lost nearly all their guns here, for nearly all the detachments and horses were killed), and of a crushing attack on the 19th Brigade and penetration of our line thereabouts. And soon afterwards the movement itself became visible, for the 14th Brigade, and then the 13th, began to give way, and one could see the trenches being evacuated on the right. The Norfolks stuck well to it on the right, and covered the retirement that was beginning; but they were taken out of my hands by Sir C. F., and told off to act as rear-guard for the brigades on their right.

The 15th Brigade had really been very lucky, and had neither been shelled nor attacked very heavily, and consequently we were pretty fresh and undamaged. I forget if we got any definite message to retire, and if so, when, but it was fairly obvious that we couldn't stay where we were much longer. The Dorsets were quite happy in Troisvilles and thereabouts, but the 9th Brigade on their left had had a very bad time, and were already beginning to withdraw, though in good order.

This being so, I sent orders to the battery of the 15th R.F.A. Brigade in my front to retire before they got cut off; and they executed it grandly, bringing up the horses at a gallop, swinging round, hooking in, and starting off at a canter as if at an Aldershot field-day, though they were under heavy shell and rifle fire all the time.

Only two horses and about two men were hit altogether, and though all these were apparently killed, the men got up after a little and were brought safely off with the Bedfords.

The K.O.S.B.'s were now falling back on us from the right, and they were strung out along the Norfolks' late position, and almost at right angles to our line, for the Germans were pressing us there, and heavy rifle fire was breaking out there and nearly in our right rear. Then I ordered the Cheshires and after them the Bedfords to retire, which they did quite calmly and in good order; and lastly came the Dorsets, very well handled by Bols and forming a rear-guard to the rest of the troops hereabouts. His machine-guns under Lieut. Wodehouse had been doing excellent work, and the shooting of both Bedfords and Dorsets had had a great effect in keeping off the German attack hereabouts.

By this time units had become a bit mixed, and lines of troops belonging to different battalions and even different brigades were retiring slowly over the open ground and under a heavy fire of shrapnel—which by the same token seemed to do extraordinarily little damage. It was difficult to give a definite point for all these troops to move on, for we had been warned against retiring through villages, as they were naturally made a cockshy of by the enemy's guns. Reumont was being already heavily bombarded, and though we had instructions to fall back south-westwards along the road to Estrées, this road passed through Reumont. I did not know how to get comfortably on to it without going through some village, so gave a general direction off the road, between it and Bertry, and struck across country, together with a number of troops on foot in various formations, all moving quite steadily and remarkably slowly.

As the shrapnel were bursting in large numbers overhead, I got the men well extended, as best I could, but some of course were hit. Just as we left the road a man in charge of an ambulance-waggon full of wounded ran up and asked what he was to do, as some infernal civilian had unhitched and gone off with the horses whilst he was attending to the wounded. Stephenson, commanding K.O.S.B.'s, was lying wounded in the waggon, but this I did not hear till afterwards. Some of the K.O.S.B.'s thereupon very gallantly harnessed themselves to the waggon and towed it along the road.

It was hard work making our way mounted across country, because of the numerous wire fences we came across, not to mention ditches and hedges. We worked rather towards Bertry, avoiding woods and boggy bits, but the line wasn't easy to keep. The Germans had an unpleasant habit of plugging bursts of four to a dozen shrapnel at one range, then another lot fifty yards on, and so on, so it was no good hurrying on, as you only came in for the next lot. Then they very nearly got us just when we had got to a hopeless-looking place—the railway, with thick fence and ditch on each side of the track and a barbed-wire fence as well, with signal wires knee high just where you expected to be able to jump down on to the track. Luckily Catley, my groom, had some wire nippers; but just as he was cutting at the wire, and we of the Brigade Staff were all standing round close by, trying to get over or through, whack came four shrapnel, one close after the other, bursting just short of us and above us—a very good shot if intentional, but I don't think they could possibly have seen us. Horses of course flew all over the place; Cadell and his horse came down, and I thought he was hit, but he only lost his cap, and his horse only got a nasty flesh wound from a bit of shrapnel in his hindquarters. Again, why none of these shrapnel hit us was most extraordinary: there we were, seven or eight of us mounted and close together, and the shells bursting beautifully with terrific and damnable cracks—yet not one of the Brigade Staff touched. Beilby's horse, by the way, also got a bullet in the quarter.

These same shrapnel hit two or three infantry standing round us, and the next thing we saw was Dillon (of the Divisional Staff) dismounted and staggering along supporting two wounded privates and hoisting them over the obstacles on to the rail track, one man hanging heavily from his neck on either side. He was streaming with sweat, and said afterwards it was the hardest job he'd ever had. Others of course helped him and his men, and we wandered along over the grass, and skirting the little woods and coppices till we got to the main road again.

As we proceeded along the road we did our best to get the troops collected into their units, getting single men together into bunches and the bunches into groups and platoons, and so on. But many of them were wounded and dog-tired, and it was hard work. Ballard and his Norfolks joined us in bits, and we heard that they had had a hard time falling back through Reumont and done very well as rear-guard. There were stories at first of their having suffered terribly and lost a lot of men; but it was not in the least true, — they had had comparatively few casualties.

The country gradually grew more and more open till by dusk—somewhere about 7 o'clock—we were traversing a huge rolling plain with open fields and only occasional farmhouses visible. The troops on the road were terribly mixed, infantry and artillery and waggons and transport all jumbled up together, and belonging not only to different brigades but even to different divisions, the main ones being of course the 5th and 3rd Divisions.

Darkness came on, and the night grew cooler and cooler, yet still we pushed on. As it got blacker, terrible blocks occurred and perpetual unintentional halts. In one place, somewhere near the Serains-Prémont road I think, we were halted for about three-quarters of an hour by a jam of waggons just ahead. I gave the Norfolks leave to worm their way through the press, but it was no use, for before they had got through the waggons moved on again and only divided the men more and more, so that they lost their formation again and were worse off than before.

Companies or bits of companies of my battalions were pretty close together, and at one time the Brigade was pretty well cohesive, but as the night wore on they got separated again and mixed up with the transport till it was quite impossible to sort them out. It was a regular nightmare, and all one could look forward to was the halt at Estrées.

The German guns had long ceased to fire, even before the sun went down, and there didn't seem to be any pursuit at all, as far as we could gather. Our men moved quite steadily and without the vestige of a sign of panic: in fact, they were much annoyed at having to fall back. But I expect the German infantry was even more tired than ours, for they had marched all through the previous night and certainly had frightfully heavy casualties during the day. Anyway they did not worry us, and we pursued our way in peace. But men and horses were desperately sleepy, and at these perpetual halts used to go to sleep and block up the road again when we moved on.

Luckily the road was as straight as a die, and one could not possibly lose it; but it was difficult to know where we were, and occasional twinkling lights in houses and cottages on the road only made our where-abouts still more deceptive.

At last we entered something that looked in the pitch darkness more like a town. It was Estrées right enough, but there were no signs of a halt, though it was 1 A.M. or so. We could not find any staff officers here, even at the solitary local inn, to give us any information, and the only rumour was that we were to march on as far as we could go. We had had no direct orders, and we did not know where the Divisional staff were, but as by this time we had pushed on and were, as far as we knew, ahead of most of the Brigade, Weatherby and I moved aside into a field full of corn stooks, unsaddled our horses, gave them a feed, and went fast asleep in the wet corn. We had meant to sleep only for half an hour, but were so

dead tired that it must have been more like
an hour and a half. And even then we were
only awakened by a battalion (I think it
was the Northumberland Fusiliers) irrupting
into our field and pulling the stooks down
for their own benefit. So we guiltily saddled
up again, thinking that the whole Brigade
must have passed us in the dark. But, as
a matter of fact, it had not.

Aug. 27th.

Daylight came at last through the damp
grey mists, and we found ourselves still in
open country, with the road thickly covered
as before with troops of all arms and, in
places by the roadside, the remains of
bivouac fires and empty boxes and bully-
beef tins, and hunks of raw meat; for the
A.S.C. finding that it was impossible to
supply the troops regularly, had wisely
dumped down their stores at intervals
alongside the road and let the men help
themselves.

This was all very well for the men in
front, but by the time we in rear had got
to the stores there was nothing left, and
we had to go hungry.

Somewhere about 4 A.M. I came on Sir

C. F. standing at the cross-roads near
Nauroy. I naturally asked him where we
were to retire on; but he had not recently
received any definite orders himself; so
after talking it over we came to the conclusion that our best line would be on
St Quentin, and we directed the men, as
they came up — 5th Division straight on,
4th Division to the right to Bellicourt, and
3rd to the left to Lehaucourt, for thus we
should get the Divisions more or less in
their right positions. Of course a vast
quantity of troops had already preceded
us, probably towards St Quentin, but that
could not be helped.

It was a long way yet to St Quentin,
about eight miles, and on the road and off
it were men, waggons, and stragglers in
every direction. The jumble of the night
had disintegrated most of the formed
bodies, and the whole thing had the appearance of a vast *débâcle*. Men moving on
singly but slowly, little bunches of three
and four men together, sometimes of the
same regiment, but oftener of odd ones; men
lying exhausted or asleep by the roadside,
or with their packs off and sitting on the
grass, nibbling at a biscuit or looking hope-

lessly before them. It was a depressing sight, and I wondered how on earth the formations would ever come together again. Officers of course were doing their best to get their own men together, but the results were small. Whenever we passed men of the 15th Brigade we collected them as far as possible into bodies; but it was very difficult to know what units men belonged to without asking them, for very many of them had long ago, on arrival at Havre and elsewhere, given their cap-badges and shoulder-names as souvenirs to women and children, and they were most difficult to identify.

A mile or two before getting into St Quentin I passed Laurence Drummond, commanding the 19th Brigade, hobbling along on foot, and offered him of course my second horse. He had got damaged somehow—by a fall, I think—and said he had his horse all right, but it hurt him less to walk than to ride.

As we approached the town the entrance had got rather blocked with troops. This was rather a good thing, as it enabled the stragglers behind to close up and find other portions of their own regiments; and, extraordinary as it seemed, whole companies had now got together and in some cases had even coagulated into battalions. I found most of the Norfolks collected together in a field by the side of the road, and a stray Bedford company or two looking quite fresh and happy.

As it was necessary to get further orders, I left Weatherby to do some more collecting and pushed on by myself into the town, where I found Rolt and some of his Staff; but he knew nothing. There was a hopeless block at this moment, so I slipped off my horse for ten minutes and had a bit of chocolate and biscuit, which were quite refreshing. Rolt was somewhat depressed, for his Brigade had lost heavily, but they too were gradually coming together. At last, in the middle of the town, I managed to collect some instructions, and was told that the 5th Division was to form up in a field near the railway station the other side of the town. There were also Staff officers at different points, calling out "5th Division this way, 3rd that," and so on; and as the men, now more or less in columns of fours, passed them, they perked up and swung along quite happily.

We were now outside the region of our

maps, so I asked my way to a stationer's, which luckily happened to be open, though it was barely 7.30 A.M., and bought all the local maps I could get hold of: they were only paper, not linen, but they proved extremely useful. And then I bought some big rings of bread and some apples, and made Catley carry them strung on the little brigade flag that S. had embroidered, and we filled up our haversacks with as much food as we could buy and carry—for the benefit of the men.

I found my way to the railway field all right, but none of the Brigade had yet arrived, so I went back to look for them. On the way I found that a number of the 13th Brigade had taken the wrong turning and were plodding right away from the town, so I had to canter after them a mile or more and turn them back. There was a lot of transport further on, on the move; and fearing that they might belong to us, whilst my horse was pretty tired, I begged a nice-looking Frenchman with a long beard—a doctor of sorts—in a motor-car, to lend me his car to catch them. This he willingly did, and drove me up to them, but they turned out to be field ambulances with orders of their own, so I came back to the railway field, leaving a man at the railway turning to turn the others and show them the way.

Gradually bits of the 15th Brigade arrived —a few Dorsets, half the Bedfords, and a few Cheshires; and to these I imparted the Staff instructions that we were to bivouac here for the night. The men had already done twenty-four miles during the night, and lay about, thankful to get a little rest. Supplies, we were told, would be issued shortly at the station, but before they came I got peremptory orders to march off at 2 o'clock, and withdraw further south to a place called Ollizy, nine miles on.

It was then 12.30 P.M., and the men had had no food since the previous morning; however, orders had to be obeyed. So I distributed my bread and apples, for which the men pressed round ravenously; and James, commanding the 2nd Manchesters, who had been in my Brigade two years previously, gave me a couple of most welcome big sandwiches and a drink. None of my staff had yet turned up; and though I was told that supplies were just going to arrive, none did arrive before we marched

E

off. Five minutes before that time the
Norfolks, who had had a rest the other
side of the town, turned up; and as the
rest of the Brigade marched off the rest of
the Dorsets marched up—rather disappointed
at having to go on at once without either
rest or rations.

Weatherby and the rest of Brigade Headquarters had trickled in by this time, and we
moved off in rear of the 13th Brigade. The
day was fairly hot by this time—luckily it
had been cool all the morning—and I expected to see whole heaps of the men fall
out exhausted; but devil a bit, they moved
on, well closed up, good march discipline,
and even whistling and singing; and for the
rest of the march I don't believe that more
than half a dozen fell out.

We expected some more fighting near
Ollizy, for a message had come through for
the 13th to push on and collar a certain
bridge before the Germans got it; but all
was peaceful, and we got to Ollizy about five
o'clock. There I had to tell off a battalion
and some guns not belonging to me to take
up a line of outposts to guard our rear (I
quite forget what the troops were, or why
they were put under me), and the Brigade

pushed on over the bridge, and through the swampy, marshy country beyond.

No halt yet, and I began to wonder whether we were expected to do yet another night march. However, after another two miles I was told to put the Brigade in bivouac round a farm and little village called Eau-court, covering our rear with another line of outposts.

There was some distant shelling during the evening; but we were too dog-tired to worry about it, though bursts of rifle fire did occur during the night, necessitating our jumping up once or twice to see what it was.

The farm was quite a good one of the usual form—*i.e.*, the living-house forming one end of a big oblong courtyard, whilst barns and lofts and cowsheds filled up the other three sides. In the middle, of course, was a mass of dirty straw and manure, and pools of stinking water in which ducks and pigs and chickens disported themselves. The people were most friendly, and supplied us with eggs and straw and a kitchen fire; but it was rather a squash, as the headquarters of an artillery brigade were already feeding there, and we didn't get dinner till very late. The men lay about in the lofts and sheds

among the farm implements and sheep, and
I should have expected them after a march
of over thirty-five miles, and no food or sleep
in the twenty-four hours, to curl up and go
to sleep at once, but they didn't; they were
quite happy and lively now that at last
they'd got their rations, and made the most
of them. I had a bed to lie on, and actually
enjoyed a wash in a real basin, but the little
bedroom was not very sweet or clean, and
I'd as soon have slept with the others on
straw in the kitchen and living-room.

Aug. 28*th.*

Next morning we were off before the sun
rose, with orders to proceed towards Noyon.
We were well up to time as regards our
place in the column, but some of the rest of
the Division were very late—probably some
counter-order had been given; anyway, we
had to wait a good extra half-hour by the
roadside. I remember that I occupied the
time in shaving myself; and as there was no
water handy, I moistened the brush in the
dew on the grass. It did fairly well—
though removing two days' growth was
rather painful, I allow.

We plodded on through the heat of the

day, in rear of the 14th Brigade, and kept our march discipline without trouble, though the number of apple- and pear-trees on the road was a great temptation. What had happened or where we were going to was a complete mystery; all that we knew was that we had had to leg it at Le Cateau, but that we were distinctly *not* downhearted; nor did the Germans seem to be pursuing. So we thought that we should probably soon get the order to turn and either take up a defensive position or advance again against the enemy—though we also knew that we must have lost a number of guns and a good many men.

Soon after we started we were asked how many waggons we required to carry damaged and footsore men, and at a certain point there were some thirty or forty waggons drawn up for that purpose. I felt rather insulted, and said so, but eventually put my pride in my pocket and said I'd have one per battalion. The officer in charge at once offered ten, but I did not accept them, and I don't think we filled even one waggon all day.

Somewhere about ten o'clock the message was passed down from the front that Sir

John French was on the roadside and wanted to see battalion commanders. I cantered on, and found him under a tree with a few of his staff. I saluted and asked for orders, but he said he only wanted to see the C.O.'s. Then he took me aside and said that he wanted to compliment and congratulate the men on their magnificent work; that we had saved the left flank of the French army, and that Joffre had begged him to tell the troops that they had saved France for the time being, and more to the same effect. I hastened, of course, to tell everybody; I think the men got their tails up well in consequence. But the British are an undemonstrative lot, and Thomas never lets his feelings show on the surface. Anyway, we were all pleased that our sacrifices hadn't been for nothing, and hoped we'd soon stop and turn round.

At Guiscard we turned into the main road to Noyon. It was very hot, and we had had no rest (except the regulation ten minutes per hour) since starting. So when we got to some nice shade on the left, and big spreading trees dotted over some fields, I turned the Brigade off the road, trans-

port and all, and we halted for an hour
and a half. We went to sleep after
luncheon, of course, and when it was time
to start I remember that Moulton-Barrett
went up to St André, who was lying fast
asleep, and shouted out, "The Germans are
on us!" Poor St André jumped to his feet
with a yell and seized his revolver; it was
a wicked joke.

The main road into Noyon was much
crowded, not only with a lot of French
cavalry going north, but a very large
number of waggons full of our own men
—of other brigades, mind you, for I don't
think there were any 15th Brigade men
there at all; but then the others had had
a harder time.

The French cavalry were a dragoon
brigade—horses looking very fit and well,
and wonderfully light equipment on them;
they do not go in for carrying half so much
on the saddle as we do—for one thing, apparently they don't consider it necessary to carry
cleaning material on the horse.

There was again a considerable squash
in Noyon, and here St André was delighted
to meet some spick-and-span young friends
of his whom he affected to treat with

great contempt, as not yet having seen a
shot fired.   Having to cross the railway
line also delayed us still more, as a long
supply-train was shunting and reshunting
and keeping the gates shut.

It was a lovely evening, and though
progress was slow, we eventually reached
Pontoise by about 7 p.m.   The country
was thickly wooded and very pretty, and
the quarters into which we got after our
sixteen-mile march were most acceptable.
Here we were told we should probably be
for several days—to rest and recuperate;
but we were beginning to have doubts
about these perpetually-promised rests
which never came off.

The Brigade Headquarters put up at a
blacksmith's shop, and the old couple here
received us with hospitality; but though
there were beds and mattresses for most
of us, there was very little to be had in
the way of vegetables or eggs or other
luxuries such as milk or butter.

Aug. 29th.

Next morning and afternoon were devoted to a little rest and cleaning up;
but I had little leisure myself, for I had

to preside over a court of inquiry for several hot and weary hours.

At 6 P.M. we suddenly received orders to move at once to Carlepont, only three miles back, and began to move by the shortest and most unblocked way. Just when we were moving off I received orders to move the other way, but with the sanction of the Divisional Staff I preferred going my own way, and went it.

The detail of the map, however, turned out to be incorrect, and I found myself at the far, instead of the near, end of the village, with a lot of transport in the narrow street between ourselves and our billets. This was hopeless, and after a prolonged jam in the dark I gave it up, put the battalions on to the pavement and down a side street, and told them to bivouac and feed where they were.

Meanwhile St André had got a kind Frenchman to give the staff some dinner, but I misunderstood the arrangement and could not find the place; so I insisted on digging out some food from our cook's waggon on the wet grass of a little park we found. And there we ate it about midnight and went to sleep in the sopping herbage. I fear my staff were not much pleased with the arrangement.

Aug. 30*th.*

Off again at 2.20 A.M., we pushed on over pretty country *viâ* Attichy to Croûtoy, a matter of eleven miles. It developed into a roasting-hot day, and the last two miles, up a very steep hill, were most trying for the transport. ' We were at the head of the column, and longed to stop in the shady little village of Croûtoy, but we had to move on beyond to some open stubble fields, where the heat was terrific.   And there we bivouacked till about midday, when we were told we might go back to Croûtoy, and did.   It was a very pretty little village with a magnificent view northwards over the Aisne.   We were very comfortably put up in General de France's château, and enjoyed there a real big bath with taps and hot water, the first genuine bath we had had since arriving at Havre.   My only *contretemps* here was that, having when half - way to Croûtoy dismounted Catley and lent his horse to a Staff officer, I never saw the horse or my kit on him again.

The Staff officer had duly sent the horse back by a sergeant of gunners, but the latter never materialized, and, strangely enough, was never heard of afterwards. So I thus lost my bivouac tent, mackintosh, lantern, and several other things, besides Catley's complete possessions, all of which were on the animal. Luckily the horse was not my own, but a spare one, as my mare Squeaky had had a sore back, and Catley was not riding her.

Aug. 31st.

Next day was awfully hot again. We were off by 7.30, and were by way of billeting at a place called Béthisy, on the south-west edge of the forest of Compiègne. We passed by the eastern edge, close by the extraordinary château of Pierrefonds, built by Viollet le Duc to the exact model of the old castle of the thirteenth century, a huge pile of turrets and battlements, like one of Gustave Doré's nightmares; and then struck across the open towards Morienval. We were a long time on the march, largely owing to the necessary habit that the Artillery have of stopping to "feed and water" when they come to water, irrespective of the hourly ten-minute halt. Then, having thus stopped the Infantry column in rear for twenty minutes, they trot on and catch up the rest of the column in front, leaving the Infantry toiling hopelessly after them, trying to fill the gap the guns leave behind them. It is bad, of course, but it is a choice of evils, for one way the Artillery suffers, the other the Infantry; but they both arrive together in the end.

I had trotted ahead to Morienval, to settle on the road, as there was a divergence of opinion on the subject, and there a kindly farmer asked me in to dinner with his family—an excellent *potage aux choux* and a succulent stew, with big juicy pears to follow, all washed down by remarkably good red *vin du pays*, I remember. There were perpetual halts on the road, which we did not understand, but soon after leaving Morienval we were abruptly ordered to turn sharp off to the left and make for Crépy. The fact was, a force of German cavalry had turned up at Béthisy, just as our billeting parties were entering it, and the latter had only just time to clear out.

Our own cavalry cleared the Germans out

of Béthisy for the time being, but we continued on to Crépy-en-Valois, and arrived there, rather done, at six o'clock — nearly eleven hours to go fifteen miles, just the sort of thing to tire troops on a very hot day, — and with numerous apparently unnecessary halts. However, we had few if any stragglers, and we made our way to some fields on the south-west of Crépy, St Agathe being the name of the district. I selected the bivouac myself, as I did not get billeting orders in time, and I preferred open fields on a hot night for the troops instead of stuffy billets in the town.

The Brigade Staff, however, occupied a little house and grounds in the suburbs, and I shall never forget arriving there with St André after seeing to the bivouac of the Brigade. There were two wine-bottles and glasses on a table on the lawn, with comfortable chairs alongside. Nearly speechless with thirst, we rushed at them. They were empty!

Sept. 1st.

The night was hot, and though I had an excellent bed I remember I could not get to sleep for ever so long. We were to

have moved off early, but the sound of
the guns not far to the north stopped us,
and orders quickly arrived for the Brigade
to go and occupy Duvy, a village a mile or
so to the west, and give what help we could
to General Pulteney's force of a Division
and a brigade, who were being attacked on
the north-west.

So we moved out rapidly and pushed out
two battalions to assist. Cavalry was reported everywhere, but it was difficult to
know which was English and which German.
The latter's patrols were fairly bold, and
single horsemen got close up to us. Broad-
wood, of the Norfolks, bowled over one of
them at 700 yards — with a rifle, it was
reported, but it was probably his machine-
gun. Meanwhile our guns on the plateau
north of Crépy supporting the 13th Brigade
did good execution, three consecutive shells
of theirs falling respectively into a squadron
of Uhlans, killing a whole gun-team, and
smashing up a gun by direct hit (27th
Brigade R.F.A.)

The two battalions working up north-west
from Duvy had just extended and were
moving carefully across country, when I received word that a large force of the enemy's

cavalry was moving on to my left rear. I did not like this, and pushed out another battalion (Norfolks) to guard my flank. But we need not have been worried, for shortly afterwards it appeared that the "hostile" cavalry was the North Irish Horse, turned up from goodness knows where.

About the same time we got a message from General Pulteney thanking us for the assistance rendered, and another one from Sir C. Fergusson telling us to continue our retirement towards Ormoy Villers as flank-guard to the rest of the Division. This we did, across country and partly on the railway —very bad going this for horses, especially as we might any moment have come across a bridge or culvert with nothing but rails across it. It is true that, if we had, we might have slipped down into the turnip fields on either side, but there were ditches and wire alongside which would have proved awkward.

We halted about Ormoy Villers station— in ruins almost, and with its big water-tank blown up,—and I put two battalions to guard the flank whilst the rest of us had a meal. Saint André had as usual managed to forage for us in the ruins, and produced a tin of sardines and some tomatoes and apples, which, with chocolate and biscuits and warm water—it was another roasting day—filled us well up. Then after a long and dusty walk through the woods we reached Nanteuil, where most of the Division had already arrived.

We had to find outposts (Dorsets and Norfolks) that night, covering a huge bit of country. I borrowed a car in order to settle how they should be put out, and ran out much too far, nearly into the enemy. It was not easy to place them, as connection through the woods was most awkward. However, we were not attacked, the German cavalry and advanced guards not having apparently come up.

I had sent Major Allason (of the Bedfords) out earlier in the day to scout northwards with a couple of mounted men, and he came back at eventide, having collared a German officer and his servant, but not brought them in. They had just been falling back at a walk with the information they had gathered, when they heard a clatter of hoofs behind them, and beheld a German cavalry officer and his man trying to gallop past them—not to attack them,—apparently bolting from some of our own cavalry. Allason, who was in front, stuck spurs into his horse and galloped after the officer and shot his horse, bringing the German down, the latter also being put out of action. Then they bound up the German's wound and took all his papers from him, which proved to be very useful, giving the location of the German cavalry and other troops. Meanwhile the officer's servant stood by, with his mouth open, doing nothing. As they couldn't carry the officer off, they left them both there and came on.

Amongst other stories, we heard here that a squadron of one of our cavalry brigades had stopped to water in a wood. A lot of German cavalry bungled on top of them, and then bolted as if the devil were after them. The row stampeded our horses, and they dashed off through the wood in all directions, leaving many of our men on foot. But their steeds were soon recovered.

Sept. 2nd.

Off again next morning at 4.15 A.M. We did rear-guard to the Division, but we had an easy time of it, the Dorsets being in rear. I had also the 27th Brigade R.F.A., the N.I.

Horse under Massereene, and 70 cyclists to help, but the Germans never pursued us or fired a shot. It was awfully hot again, but we had not far to go—only eleven miles—into Montgé. There we arrived at 10.45 A.M., and should have been there much sooner if it had not been for some of the Divisional Train halting to water on the way.

Montgé is a nice little village on a hillside, almost within sight of Paris, which is only about twenty-five miles off; and on a clear day one can, I believe, see the Eiffel Tower and Montmartre. We could not make out why we were always thus retiring without fighting, and imagined it was some deep-laid plan of Joffre's that we perhaps were to garrison Paris whilst the French turned on the Germans. But no light was vouch-safed to us. Meanwhile the retirement was morally rather bad for our men, and the stragglers increased in numbers.

The Brigade Headquarters billeted in a tiny house marked by two big poplars on the main road. The proprietor, a stout peasant —I think he was the Maire—received us very civilly, but his questions as to our retirement were difficult to answer. How-ever, we didn't trouble him long, and were off next morning by 5.30 acting as flank-guard again.

Sept. 3rd.

It was hotter than ever over those parched fields, and the march was complicated, for when we had reached Trilbardon down a narrow leafy path, past a bridge over the Marne which an R.E. officer was most anxious to blow up at once, we were told to act as rear-guard again. For this we had to wait till all the troops had passed through the little streets, and then we followed. We overtook a good many stragglers, and these we hustled along, insisting on their getting over the other side of the Marne before the main bridges were blown up. We were responsible for leaving no one behind, but I'm afraid that several were left, as they had fallen out and gone to sleep under hedges and were not seen; and one K.O.S.B. man was suffering so violently from pains in his tummy that he at first refused to stir, and said he didn't care if he *was* taken prisoner. There were a considerable number of these tummy cases on the way—hot sun and un-ripe apples had, I fancy, a good deal to do with them.

At Esbly we halted, gratefully, in the shade for an hour; it was a nice little town, but strangely empty, for nearly all the inhabitants had fled.

We put up for the night round Mont Pichet, a beastly little hamlet, with the Cheshires and one company Bedfords finding the outposts. The Brigade Headquarters billeted round a horrible little house, surrounded by hundreds of ducks and chickens, which ran in and out all over the place till it stank most horribly. There was only one room which wasn't absolutely foul, and that I took. The others slept in the open. I wish I had.

I went to visit the outposts by myself; and my wretched pony, Gay, refused to cross a little stream about two feet broad and two inches deep. Nothing would induce her to cross it, so I had to send her back and do it all on foot, beyond a village called Chevalrue and back. By the time I got back, late, hot, and hungry, I must have done four miles on foot.

Sept. 4th.

Having been told we should be here for at least a day to rest, we received orders, I need hardly say, at 7 next morning, to be ready to move immediately. However, it was rather a false alarm, as, except for a Divisional "pow-wow" on general subjects, at 10 A.M. at Bouleurs, we had little to do all day, and did not move till 11.50 P.M. There had been an alarm in the afternoon, by the way, of German cavalry advancing, and I reinforced the Bedfords with another company, and got two howitzers ready to support, but the "Uhlans" did not materialize.

I might here mention, by the way, that all German cavalry, whether Lancers or not, went by the generic name of Uhlans. But it was perhaps not surprising, as all the hostile cavalry, even Hussars, had lances. They were, however, extraordinarily unhandy with them, and our own cavalry had a very poor opinion of their prowess and dash.

Sept. 5th.

The Divisional Orders for the march were complicated, and comprised marching in two columns from different points and meeting about ten miles off. Also, the collecting of my outposts and moving to a left flank was complicated. But it went off all right, and we marched gaily along in the cool night and effected the junction at Villeneuve. Thence on through a big wood with a network of rides, where the two officers who were acting as guides in front went hopelessly astray and took the wrong turning. The leading battalion was, however, very shortly extricated and put on the right road, and after passing Tournans we halted, after a sixteen-mile march, at a magnificent château near Gagny (Château de la Monture) at 7.30 A.M.

Here we made ourselves extremely comfortable in the best bedrooms of M. Boquet, of the Assurance Maritime, Havre, and sent him a letter expressing our best thanks. Up to 6 P.M. we slept peacefully, with no orders to disturb us, but then they arrived and gave us great joy, for we were to march at 5 A.M., not southwards, but northwards again.

Sept. 6th.

What had happened, or why we were suddenly to turn against the enemy after ten days of retreat, we could not conceive; but the fact was there, and the difference in the spirits of the men was enormous.

They marched twice as well, whistling and singing, back through Tournans and on to Villeneuve. Here we had orders to halt and feed, but the halt did not last long, for a summons to the 5th Division Headquarters (in a hot and stuffy little pot-house) arrived at 1 P.M., and by 2 we were marching on through the Forêt de Crécy to Mortcerf. It was frightfully hot and dusty, and the track through the forest was not easy to find. Although I had issued stringent orders about the rear of one unit always dropping a guide for the next unit (if not in sight) at any cross-roads we came to, something went astray this time, and half the Brigade turned up at one end of the village of Mortcerf, whilst the other half came in at the other. We were on advanced guard at the time, and so increasing the frontage like this did no harm; but it caused rather a complication in the billets we proceeded to allot.

A delightful little village it was, and the Maire, in whose house we put up, was extremely kind; but by the time I had covered the front with outposts and ridden back, very hot and tired, General Smith Dorrien turned up, and announced that we were to push on in an hour. He was, by the way, very complimentary about the way in which the 15th Brigade had behaved all through, and cast dewdrops upon us with both hands. It was very pleasant, but I was rather taken aback, for I genuinely did not think that we had done anything particularly glorious in the retreat. However, it appeared that the authorities considered that the Brigade was extremely well disciplined and well in hand—for which the praise was due to the C.O.'s and not to me—and were accordingly well pleased.

So we made a hurried little meal at the Maire's house, and Madame threw us delicious pears from a first-floor window as we rode away.

We had not far to go in the dusk, only two or three miles on to the turning which led to La Celle. The Dorsets were pushed on into and beyond La Celle, in rather complicated country—for there was a deep valley and a twisting road beyond; but the few Uhlans in the village bolted as they entered it, and no further disturbances occurred in our front. On our right, however, there was heavy firing, for the 3rd Division had come across a good many of the enemy at Faremoutiers, and at 9.30, and again at 11.30, general actions seemed to be developing. But they died away, and we slept more or less peacefully on a stubble field with a few sheaves of straw to keep us warm. Perpetual messengers, however, kept on arriving with orders and queries all night long, and our sleep was a broken one.

Sept. 7th.

We awoke with the sun, feeling—I speak for myself—rather touzled and chippy, and waited a long time for the orders to proceed. The cooks' waggon turned up with the Quartermaster - Sergeant and breakfast — and still we didn't move. Eventually we fell in and moved off at noon—a hot day again—very hot, in fact, as we strung along on a narrow road in the deep and wooded valley. Very pretty country it was; but what impressed itself still more on me was the gift of some most super - excellent "William" pears by a farmer's wife in a tiny village nestling in the depths—real joy on that thirsty day.

There were still some Uhlans left in the woods, and I turned a couple of Norfolk

companies off the road to drive them out.
Some of our artillery had also heard of
them, and a Horse battery dropped a few
shells into the wood to expedite matters;
but I regret to say the only bag, as far as
we could tell, was one of our own men
killed and another wounded by them.

At Mouroux we halted for a time, and
then pushed on, rather late, to Boissy le
Châtel — the delay being caused by the
motor-bikist carrying orders to us missing, by some mischance, our Headquarters
altogether—though we were within a few
hundred yards of Divisional Headquarters,
and had reported our whereabouts — and
going on several miles to look for us.

We were now again the advanced guard of
the Division, and had to find outposts for
it a mile beyond. It is always rather a
grind having to ride round the outposts
after a long day, but one can't sleep in
peace till one is satisfied that one's front
is properly protected, so it has to be done;
and as the Brigade Staff is limited, the
Staff Captain allotting the billets, and the
Brigade Major seeing that all the troops
arrive safely, one generally has to do these
little excursions by oneself. On the road

I came across Hubert Gough, commanding
the 3rd Cavalry Brigade, in a motor, cheery
as ever, with his cavalry somewhere on our
right flank keeping touch with us. We
put up in a little deserted château in Boissy
le Châtel, but it was overcrowded with trees
and bushes and very stuffy.

Sept. 8th.

Next morning we had, before starting,
the unpleasant duty to perform of detailing
a firing-party to execute a deserter. I
forget what regiment he belonged to (not
in our brigade), but he had had rotten luck
from his point of view. He had cleared
out and managed to get hold of some civilian
clothes, and, having lost himself, had asked
the way of a gamekeeper he met. The
gamekeeper happened to be an Englishman,
and what was more, an old soldier, and
he promptly gave him up to the authorities
as a deserter.

We left at 7.25 A.M. as the last brigade
in the Division. I might mention here that,
for billeting, the ground for the Division
was divided into "Brigade Areas," each
area to hold not only an Infantry Brigade
but one or two Artillery Brigades, a Field

Ambulance, and generally a company of R.E., and occasionally some other odds and ends, such as Divisional Ammunition Column, Train, Irish Horse, Cyclists, &c., and for all these we had to find billets. The troops billeted in these areas varied in composition nearly every day. It was very hard work for the Staff Captain (Moulton-Barrett), whose proper job would normally have been limited to the 15th Brigade; but he and Saint André, who both worked like niggers, somehow always managed to do it satisfactorily. It would have turned my hair grey, I know, to stuff away a conflicting crowd of troops of different arms into an area which was always too small for them. But M.-B. would sit calmly on his horse amid the clamour of inexperienced subalterns and grasping N.C.O.'s, and allot the farms and streets in such a way that they always managed to get in somehow—though occasionally I expect the conditions were not those of perfect comfort. We were lucky in the weather, however, and many times troops bivouacked in the open in comparative ease when a rainy night would have caused them extreme discomfort.

It was not always easy to find billets even

for our own Brigade Staff, for though we
were a small unit, comparatively, we had
a good number of horses and half a dozen
vehicles; and besides this, we had to have
a decent room or place for the Signal section,
and rig up a wire for them to work in connection with the Divisional Headquarters
or other troops. In this Cadell was excellent,
and we rarely had a breakdown. Sometimes, of course, we were too far off to get
a wire fixed in time, and then we had
recourse to our Signal "push-bikists"—no
motor cyclists being on our establishment.
The Signal companies, by the way, had
only been completely organized a month
or two before the war, and what we should
have done without them passes my imagination, for they were quite invaluable, and
most excellently organized and trained.

And sometimes when, after all this work,
we had settled down into billets for the
night, an order would come to move on at
once. Fresh orders had then hurriedly to
be written, and despatched by the orderly
of each unit (who was attached to our headquarters) to his respective unit, giving the
time at which the head of the unit was to
pass a given point on the road so as to

dovetail into its place in the column in the dark, and all with reference to what we were going to do, whether the artillery or part of it was to be in front or in rear, what rations were to be carried, arrangements for supply, position of the transport in the column, compositions of the advanced or rear-guard, &c., &c. It sounds very complicated, and still more so when you have to fit in not only your own brigade but all the miscellaneous troops of your "Brigade Area." But Weatherby had reduced this to a fine art, and, after all, we had had heaps of practice at it; so orders were short and to the point, and issued in really an extraordinarily short time.

To return. Our march that day was through pretty country, with fighting always going on just ahead of us or on both flanks, but we were never actually engaged. At Doue we halted for an hour or so, and then received orders to push out a battalion to hold the high ground in front. But when we had got there we only found a panorama stretching out all round, dotted with troops, and our guns firing from all sorts of unseen hiding-places, with the enemy well on the run in front of us. Soon the order came for us to push on, and we moved forward through Mauroy, down a steep hill into St Cyr and St Ouen, pretty little villages in a cleft in the ground, across the Petit Morin river and up a beastly steep hill on the other side.

Then came a "pow-wow" in a stiff shower of rain, and on again slowly over the plateau, in a curious position, for there was a big fight going on amid some burning villages in the plain far on our left — I don't know what Division—probably the 4th—and a smaller fight parallel to us on the right, not two miles off; and we were marching calmly along the road in column.

Then a longer halt, whilst we got closer touch with the 14th Brigade on our right. It was a tangled fight there; for when we pushed forward some cyclists in that direction they were unintentionally fired on by the East Surrey; and the latter, who had rounded up and taken about 100 of the enemy prisoners, mostly cavalry, were just resting whilst they counted them, when some of our own guns lobbed some shells right into the crowd, and five German officers and about fifty of the prisoners escaped in the confusion.

A little farther on, near Charnesseuil,

we got orders to billet for the night there, and the Brigade Headquarters moved on to Montapeine cross-roads. Here there was a good deal of confusion, stray units of several divisions trying to find their friends, and the cross-roads blocked by a small body of sixty-three German prisoners. We got the place cleared at last, and the Staff occupied an untidy, dirty, unfurnished house and grounds at the corner. It had been used by the enemy the night before, and they had luckily brought great masses of straw into the house.

I stowed away the prisoners in the stables —great big, docile, sheepish-looking men of the Garde-Schützen-Bataillon (2nd and 4th companies) and machine-gun battery attached. I talked to several of them, and they said that the battalion had lost very heavily and there were hardly any officers left. One of the latter, Fritz Wrede by name, I found wounded and lying on the straw in a dark room in the basement. Other wounded were being brought in here, and all complained of feeling very cold, although the evening was quite warm. I made some men heap straw on them, which was an improvement — but I believe that wounded always do feel cold.

Wrede had a bullet through the shoulder, but was not bad, so I got him to sign a paper to say he would not try to escape—otherwise he might have made trouble. Our men, as usual, were more than kind to the prisoners, and insisted on giving them their own bread and jam — though the Germans had already been given a lot of biscuit. I remember being struck with the extreme mild-seemingness of all the prisoners, and wondering how such men could have been capable of such frightful brutalities as they had been in Belgium—they looked and behaved as if they wouldn't have hurt a fly.

Sept. 9th.

Next morning we moved off at 7.30 and went *viâ* Saacy across the Marne to Merz, and thence up an extremely steep and bad road through the woods. It was a very hot day, and as there was no prospect of getting the transport up I left it behind at Merz, meaning to send it round another way when the road was clear. Firing was going on to the left front, and we halted for a council of war with the Divisional Staff, which was immediately in front of us.

The 14th Brigade was apparently hung up

G

somewhere to our left front and couldn't get
on, so we were sent on to help them take
the high ground towards the Montreuil road.
They were, we were told, already in possession of Hill 189; but when we emerged from
the woods there was a Prussian battery on
the hill. There did not seem to be any men
with it, as far as we could see, and it was not
firing. But we made a good target, and not
more than a battalion had got clear when
the "deserted" battery opened fire and
lobbed a shell or two into the Bedfords
and Cheshires.

They only lost a man or two killed and
wounded; but a Howitzer battery with us,
which was already on the look-out, came
into action at once and speedily silenced the
German guns for the time being.

Bols, who was leading, reported that the
hill was attackable—it was really only a rise
in the ground,—and after a reconnaissance
I gladly issued orders. So the Norfolks
and Dorsets proceeded to attack in proper
form, whilst I sent the Bedfords round to
the right towards Bézu to try and take
the rise in flank. The 14th Brigade were
meanwhile somewhere on the left, and we
got touch with them after a time; but they

could not get forward, as a number of big guns from much further off kept up a heavy fire, and there was a body of infantry hidden somewhere as well, to judge from the number of bullets that came over and into us.

That was rather a trying afternoon. Dorsets and Norfolks were held up about half a mile from Hill 189, and I went forward to Bézu with the Bedfords to try to get them on to the flank. Thorpe and his company got forward into a wood, but lost a number of men in getting there; and the lie of the ground did not seem to justify my sending many more to help him, as the space up to the wood was swept by a heavy fire. Just about this time poor Roe of the Dorsets, who had taken some of his company into this wood, was shot through the head — as was also George, one of his subalterns.

Meanwhile those horrible big guns from somewhere near Sablonnières were giving us a lot of trouble, and knocked out also several of the Cheshires, who had been sent by the Divisional Commander towards the left to support the 14th Brigade. The latter — (I went to see Rolt, the Brigadier,

but there was little we could combine)—
seemed at one moment to be a little unhappy, as they were enfiladed from Chanoust
on their left; but the Dorsets had worked
carefully forward on their tummies, and
with the Norfolks held a low ridge well to
the front, whence, though they could not
get forward themselves, they could do the
enemy a good deal of damage. So the 14th
Brigade stuck it out, and we kept up the
game till dusk, when we dug ourselves in
a little further back and posted outposts.

I might add that when Weatherby and I
went forward to see Bols and Ballard,
Weatherby had bad luck, for his horse
was shot in the body whilst he was leading
him, and died that night.

Meanwhile the 9th Brigade of the 3rd
Division was on our right, under Shaw, and
although his Lincolns, or some of them,
had got into the wood, and we tried a combined movement, they also got hung up
there and we could not get on.

The Germans certainly fought this rear-
guard action remarkably well. We did not
know at the time that it was a rear-guard
action, for we thought a whole corps might
be occupying a strong position here and

intending to fight next day. But no more fighting took place that night, and by next morning they had cleared out.

The Germans had evidently only just left Bézu, for on my going to see M'Cracken (commanding 7th Brigade) there, I found him in a house with the remains of an unfinished (German) meal, including many half-empty bottles, on the table. Then we managed to get some supper in another house, and were nearly turned out of it by a subaltern of General Hamilton's staff, who, seeing a light in the window, thought he would save himself the trouble of hunting for another house for his General, and announced that it was required for the 3rd Divisional Staff. I was inclined to demur at first and sit tight; but the ever-useful Saint André, to save trouble, hurried out and secured another house for us; as a matter of fact it was better and bigger than the first one, and would have suited the Divisional Staff much better.

After issuing orders for to-morrow's attack or march we flung ourselves down dead tired, and were awakened ten minutes afterwards by a summons from General Hamilton to come and see him at once, as he was going to hold a pow-wow on the situation. I found him in a tiny, poky little attic, and there we waited for three-quarters of an hour whilst Rolt was being sent for. Two hours did this pow-wow last, and we had to write and issue fresh orders in consequence. Just as they had been sent out and we had flung ourselves down again for a little sleep, an entirely new set of orders arrived from the 5th Division, and for the third time we had to think out and write and distribute a fresh set of orders. By that time it was 12.30 A.M., and we were to move at 3.45 A.M., which meant getting up at 2.30. Two hours broken sleep that night was all we got—and lucky to get it.

Sept. 10*th.*

Off at 3.45 A.M., we moved out in careful fashion towards Haloup, in the direction of Montreuil. But our scouts reported all clear, and in very truth the Germans had left. What was more, they had left that field battery on Hill 189 behind them, surrounded by about twenty or more corpses and a quantity of ammunition.

It was a damp day, and progress was slow, as it was not at all certain where the enemy was. At Denizy, a small village on the way, we were told that a German general, with his staff, had received a severe shock there the day before by an unexpected British shell dropping on his headquarters whilst he was at luncheon. He had jumped up with a yell and bolted up the hill, but was driven down again by another shell which landed close by. He was reported to have died almost at once, but whether from fright or not was not quite clear.

When near Germigny we espied a German column in the distance, and shelled it heavily with the 61st howitzer battery attached to us (Major Wilson), causing it to bolt in all directions. The 3rd Cavalry Brigade now turned up in our front (Hubert Gough's), and with the 5th (Chetwode's) hustled the enemy along. We were advanced guard again, and it was difficult to get on, for the Divisional Commander kept sending messages from behind asking me why the deuce I wasn't going faster, whilst Gough was sending me protests from the front that I was treading on his heels, and not giving him time to clear up the situation!

We halted for some time the other side of Germigny, and then pushed on to Gandelu, a large village in a cleft of the hills, from the heights in front of which the German artillery might have made it extremely unpleasant for us. But none were there, nor were there any at Chézy, which would have made a perfect defensive position for them, with a glacis-like slope in all directions.

On the other side of Gandelu, in the wood, we came across the first signs of the German bolt. A broken motor-car was lying in the stream, and dead horses and men were lying about, whilst every now and then we passed two or three of our troopers with a dozen German prisoners in tow.

As we moved up the steep hill towards Chézy, we came across packs, rifles, and kit of all sorts flung away, broken-down waggons, more dead Germans, and, at last, on a whole convoy of smashed waggons, their contents mostly littered over the fields and road, and groups of our horsemen beaming with joy. The 3rd Cavalry Brigade had rounded up this convoy with their Horse Artillery, scuppered or bolted most of the escort, and captured the rest. Besides this, they had attacked a whole cavalry division and scattered it to the winds.

Their first lot of prisoners numbered 348, and their second 172.

We halted near the convoy for our usual ten minutes, and examined it with much satisfaction. There were all sorts of things in the waggons—food and corn, to which I allowed our men to help themselves, for our horses were short of oats and our men of rations, and some of the tinned meats, "gulasch" and "blutwurst," were quite excellent and savoury, much more so than our everlasting bully beef. Other waggons were full of all sorts of loot—cases of liqueur and wine, musical instruments, household goods, clothing, bedding, &c., trinkets, clocks, ribbons, and an infinite variety of knick-knacks, many of which one would hardly have thought worth taking. But the German is a robber at heart, and takes everything he can lay his hands on. There was also a first-rate motor-car, damaged, by the side of the road, and in it were a General's orders and decorations, and 100 rifle cartridges (Mauser) with soft-nosed bullets. To make certain of this I kept one of the cartridges and gave it to Sir C. Fergusson. I think these were about the only things (besides food) which we took from the whole convoy, though many of the other things would have been well worth taking. The men were very good, and did not attempt even to leave the ranks till allowed by me to take the corn and food.

A short way on was the dirty village of Chézy, and here we found a heap of cavalry and many of the 3rd Division. So we branched off to the left in a frightfully heavy ten minutes' shower, and marched away to St Quentin—marked as a village, but really only a farmhouse in a big wood. As we approached the wood Headlam's guns began to shell it in order to clear it of possible hostile troops, and continued until I sent back to say that the shells were preventing us from going on ; then he eased off.

We halted near St Quentin for half an hour, and then came a message to say we were to billet there. It was impossible to billet a whole brigade in one farmhouse, and that none too large. So we told off different fields for the battalions to bivouac in, and occupied the farm ourselves, first sending out cyclists to clear the wood, as there were rumoured to be parties of Uhlans in it.

It was a grubby farm with not much water, but we made the best of it, and settled down for the night. A starved-looking priest was also sleeping there, and he told me his story.

He and a fellow-priest, an Aumônier from Paris, had been on their way to join the French unit to which they had been allotted for ambulance purposes, when they fell into German hands and were treated as prisoners. The priest was robbed by a sergeant of 1200 francs, his sole possessions, and both he and the Aumônier were beaten black and blue, forced to march carrying German knapsacks, and kept practically without food or drink. After three days the Aumônier succumbed to ill usage and died, and the priest only managed to escape because his captors were themselves on the run.

The priest also told us that there were some British prisoners in the column, and that the Germans behaved perfectly brutally to them, kicking them, starving them, and forcing them to carry German knapsacks.

Sept. 11*th.*

Next morning we did not move off till 9.25, for the supplies to the Brigades did not arrive as soon as we expected, and hence the column was late in starting. We dawdled along, forming the rear brigade, in cool weather, and nothing in particular happened beyond reports coming in from the front that the Germans were quite demoralised. It came on to pour as we left Chouy, and at Billy we parked the transport and prepared to billet there. But it was already chokeful of other troops, and more than half our brigade would have had to bivouac in the sopping fields. So we pushed on to St Remy, and, evacuating some cavalry and making them move on to some farms a bit ahead,—including Massereene and his North Irish Horse, who, I fear, were not much pleased at having to turn out of their comfortable barns, — we billeted there, headquarters being taken up in the Curé's house. Even here his poor little rooms had been ransacked, drawers and tables upset and their contents littered over the floor, and everything of the smallest value stolen by the Germans.

Sept. 12th.

Off at 5 A.M., we did only a short march as far as the Ferme de l'Epitaphe, a huge farm standing by itself in a vast and dreary plain of ploughed fields. Here we halted in pouring rain all day, expecting orders to go on. But we eventually had to billet there, with the Divisional Headquarters, and though we could only put up the Bedfords and the Cheshires there was a terrific squash. The Dorsets and Norfolks were sent back to billet at Nampteuil, a village a mile or so back, but even here there was some confusion, as the 14th Brigade had meanwhile arrived and begun to billet there. They were, however, sent back likewise to Chrisy, and the whole Division passed a most uncomfortable night. The rain never ceased from pouring, and a gale sprang up, which made matters worse. We slept in a loft with a number of Cheshire and Bedford officers, and didn't get dinner till past nine. Some gunner officers turned up, with no food at all, and we fed them ; but there wasn't much at the best of times, for we had no rations and had to depend on the contents of our Mess basket, which consisted only of Harvey sauce, knives and forks, an old ham-bone, sweet biscuits, and jam.

Sept. 13*th.*

It was fine in the morning, but the farm-yard was ankle-deep in water and slush, and the sky was leaden with lurid clouds in the east, when we started at 4.10 A.M. We pushed on slowly in column for the few miles to Serches, and there we halted at the cross-roads on the top of the plateau and parked the brigade whilst the situation was cleared up by troops in front. Shells began to drop unpleasantly near us, and a couple of field batteries which got into action just in front of us, together with a "cow-gun"[1] (60 lb.) battery, only drew the hostile fire still more. They were pretty big shells, Black Marias mostly, and the heavy battery being right out in the open suffered somewhat severely, losing eight horses and a few men killed and wounded by one shell alone.

So we prudently scattered the battalions a bit, and the field batteries limbered up and walked slowly back under cover of a slope. But the cow-guns had one gun disabled, and though they also moved back and got again

---

[1] So called because similar guns in the South African war had been drawn by oxen.

into action they were evidently spotted and had rather a poor time.

Just about then, too, the transport of the 13th Brigade, which was necessarily following the infantry over the crest towards Sermoise, were noticed by the enemy, and a few shells over them killed and disabled a number of waggon-horses and men, making a very nasty mess in the road.

There we sat all day whilst the sun came out and dried us a bit. But we were not very happy at luncheon; for though hungry and with plenty to eat now, those beastly shells came nearer and nearer us, till our bully and biscuit lost their charm entirely. At last we got up, plates in hand, and moved with dignity out of range, or, rather, more under cover.

The Cheshires had meanwhile discovered a curious cave in the hillside which sheltered the whole battalion (though, in truth, the latter was not large, only 450 men or so), whilst the other battalions were well out of sight in the folds of the ground.

The shadows grew longer and longer, and we rigged up some comfortable little shelters in the coppice for the night, thinking we should bivouac where we were. But at 6 I

was sent for to Divisional Headquarters at
Serches, and told to reconnoitre the road
towards the Aisne — only a mile or two
ahead. This I did in a motor-car, and
returned in time for dinner; but we had
barely got through it, about 8, when marching orders came to the effect that we were
to push on and cross the Aisne by rafts to-
night, and the sooner the better.

So we moved off with some difficulty in
the dark, for there were no connecting roads
with the halting-places of the battalions, and
got on to the main road, whence all was
plain sailing, down to the Moulin des Roches,
an imaginary mill on the river bank. Over
some sloppy pasture fields in dead silence,
and we found ourselves on the bank, with
a darker shadow plashing backwards and
forwards over the river in our front, and
some R.E. officers talking in whispers.

The actual crossing of the Brigade was a
long job, and had to be carefully worked
out. The raft held sixty men at a time,
or thirty men and three horses; but as
horses on a raft in the dead of night were
likely to cause a fuss, we left them behind,
to follow on in the morning, and crossed
without them, — four and a half hours it

took; and whilst the men were crossing
we tried to get a bit of sleep on the wet
bank. It was not very successful, as it
was horribly cold and we had no blankets.
The staff crossed last of all, and we landed
in a wood on the far side, in a bog but
thinly covered with cut brushwood, and
full of irritating, sharp, and painful tree-
stumps.

Sept. 14*th.*

When we were across it was difficult to
discover the battalions asleep in the fields,
and when we had found them and it was
time to start it was difficult to wake
them. However, we moved off just as it
was getting light; but it was not easy to
find the way, for there was no path at
first. We had orders to go *viâ* Bucy-le-
Long to Sainte Marguerite, and found the
villages right enough, for they were close
together. But as we moved into Sainte
Marguerite, with a good many other troops
in front of us, we became aware that there
was an unnecessary number of bullets flying about, and that our fellows in front
were being held up.

The village was held by the 12th Brigade

H

(4th Division), and the 14th Brigade was
somewhere on our right. The Dorsets were
our leading battalion, and they were pushed
on to help the 12th, and filled a gap in
their line on the hill above the village front
at the eastern end. But there we stuck
for a long time. The enemy's artillery had
meanwhile opened on us, and shells began
to crash overhead and played the devil with
the tiles and the houses. But they did not
do us much harm.

We now received orders to move on to
Missy (not a mile off to the right) and clear
the Chivres ridge of the enemy and push on
to Condé and take that if possible—rather
a "large order." The difficulty was to get
to Missy, for the road thither was spattered
with bullets, and shells were bursting all
along it. However, by dint of careful work
we moved out bit by bit, cutting through
the gardens and avoiding the road, and
taking advantage of a slight slope in the
ground by which we could sneak to the
far side of the little railway embankment
which led to Missy Station.

It took a long time, and I made what
proved to be the serious mistake of stay-
ing to the end in order to see the whole

Brigade clear of Sainte Marguerite. I ought really to have gone ahead with the first party to reconnoitre; for just as we were starting after the rear company I stopped to write a message to the Division in answer to one which had just arrived, and at that moment a hellish shrapnel, machine-gun, and rifle fire was opened, not only on the village but on all the exits therefrom, and this fire lasted for nearly two hours. One simply could not make the attempt; it would have been certain death. And so we had to sit in the tiny courtyard of one of the houses, with our backs against the wall, and listen to the inferno overhead, whilst the proprietor's wife plied us with most acceptable roast potatoes and milk.

I wrote a lot of messages during those two hours, but whether they all got through or not I do not know: some of the messengers never came back. Colonel Seely turned up at one moment—from General Headquarters, I think—demanding information. This I supplied, and made use of him to take some of my orders back; it really was quite a new sensation giving orders to a recent Secretary of State for War.

At one time two or three artillery waggons

appeared in the little main street and remained there quietly for a bit under a heavy fire, but only losing a man or two slightly wounded. Then suddenly there was a loud crack overhead, and half a dozen horses were lying struggling and kicking on the ground, with great pools of blood forming in the road and four or five prostrate men in them. It was a horrible sight for us, for the shell had burst just opposite the gate of our courtyard. But the gunners behaved magnificently, and a farrier sergeant gave out his orders as quietly and unconcernedly as if he had been on parade. I took his name with a view to recommendation, but regret that I have forgotten it by now.

We also had some very unpleasant shaves at this time in our own courtyard. Twice did a shell burst just above the house and drive holes in the roof, bringing down showers of tiles; the second time practically all the tiles fell on me and nearly knocked me down. I do not know why they did not hurt me more—luckily the house was a low one; but they merely bruised my back.

At last, in a lull, we managed to get away, and sneaked out at a run—through a yard

and back garden, behind a farm, out at the
back behind a fold in the ground, then across
a wide open field and on to the low railway
embankment, behind which we ducked, and
made our way to the little station of Missy
and up behind some scattered houses to near
the church.

Here, after some trouble, we got the
commanding officers together, and arranged
to push on and attack the wooded ridge
above the town. The force was rather
mixed. I had met Rolt (commanding the
14th Brigade) on the way, and we had
settled that I should collect whatever of
his men I could get together in Missy and
join them to my attacking party. The
difficulty was that it was already getting
late—4.30 P.M.—and that there was insuffi-
cient time for a thorough reconnaissance,
though we did what we could in that direction. However, my orders from the Divisional Commander had been to take the
ridge, and I tried to do it. I had got together three companies of the Norfolks,
three of the Bedfords, two Cheshires (in
reserve), two East Surreys (14th Brigade),
and two Cornwalls (13th Brigade, who had
arrived *via* the broken bridge at Missy and

some rafts hastily constructed there)—twelve companies altogether.

But when they pushed forward it became very difficult, for there turned out to be too many men for the space. What I had not known was that, though they could advance up a broad clearing to more than half-way up the hill, this clearing was bounded on both flanks, as it gradually drew to a point, by high 6-feet wire netting just inside the wood, so that the men could not get properly into the wood, but were gradually driven in towards the point, where the only entrance to the wood occurred.

Luckily the Germans had not noticed this either — or there would have been many more casualties than there were. As it was, a company of the East Surrey and another one (Allason's) of the Bedfords did get through to the top of the wood and on to the edge of the open plateau; but this I did not hear of till later. When the greater part of the force had got through the opening into the wood they found a few Germans there and drove them back, killing some. Then they surged on to a horse-shoe-shaped road further on in the wood, and some men lost their direction and began firing in front of them at what they thought were Germans. But they were others of our own, and these began firing back, also without knowing that they were their friends. Consequently, although casualties were few, an unpleasant situation arose, and numbers of men turned about and retired down the hill into Missy, saying that our artillery was firing into them. This may have been true, for some shells were bursting over the wood; but whether they were English or German I do not know to this day.

Anyhow, the stream of men coming back increased. They fell back into the village, and then came some certainly German shells after them. For an unpleasant quarter of an hour the little sloping village of Missy was heavily shelled by shrapnel; but the walls of the houses were thick, and though of course there were a certain number of casualties, they were not serious as long as the men kept close to the south side of the walls. Beilby (our Veterinary officer) for some reason would keep to the wrong side of the street and was very nearly killed, the fuse of a shell landing with a whump on a door not two feet in front of him, and a shrapnel bullet going through his skirt pocket; but he was not touched. The shrapnel were in bursts of four, and luckily Moulton-Barrett noticed it, for he calmly held up the stream of men till the fourth shell had burst, and then let as many as possible past the open space there till the next bunch arrived, when he stopped them behind cover, — just like a London policeman directing traffic.

I remember one man falling, as we thought dead, close to where the Staff were standing. But he groaned, and Weatherby ran to pick him up. There was, however, no wound of any sort on him, and after a minute he got up and went on. I think he must have been knocked down by the wind of a shell — for he certainly was as much astonished as we were at finding no damage on himself.

By this time I had given orders that the troops were to retire to their previous positions in and near the village, and it was getting dusk.

Luard (Norfolks) and a party of twenty-five men were well ahead in the wood, and received the order to retire, for Luard was heard shouting it to his men. But nothing has since been heard of him, and I much regret to say that he was either taken prisoner with most of his men, or, more probably, killed.

A message now came down from the plateau saying that some East Surreys and Bedfords were still up in the wood, and should they retire or hold on? As it was nearly dark and I consequently could not support them—for if the men could not get through the wire-netting in daylight they could hardly do so at night—I told them to retire. I gave this order after I had consulted Rolt, who was somewhere west of the village; but even if Rolt had not been there I should have given it, for it would have been impossible to reinforce them adequately in the circumstances.

So I issued orders for an early reconnaissance and attack next morning, to be led by the Norfolks; and the troops covered their front with sentries and bivouacked in and round the village. We were all short of food that night, for none of our supply carts, and not even a riding-horse, had come with us. But all or most of the men had an "iron ration" on them, and this they consumed, with the "unexpired" portion of their previous day's ration.

The Bedfords took up their position along the railway to the west, Cheshires on the right, Norfolks right front of village, D.C.L.I. left front.

As for the Staff, we retired to a farm called La Bizaie, three-quarters of a mile south of Missy, and close to the river, and took up our quarters there. There was not a whole pane of glass in the house, for it had been heavily bombarded — being empty, except for a few wounded — during the day, and great craters had been formed close by the walls by the Black Marias. But except at one corner of the roof of an outhouse, no damage had been done to the buildings—except the broken glass.

It was a very old farmhouse, as we found out afterwards, part of it dating back to 1200 and something. Curiously enough, there was a photograph of an English Colonel (of the R.A.M.C.) on the sideboard— a friend, so the farm servants told us, of the owner, whose name I have forgotten. The buildings were very superior to the ordinary farm type, and more like a comfortable country house than one would expect, but there were plenty of barns as well, and some pigs and chickens running about.

We bought, murdered, and ate an elderly

chicken, but otherwise there was devilish little to eat except a store of jam, and we had only a very few biscuits and no bread.

Sept. 15th.

After writing out orders for the attack next day we went to bed, dog-tired; and

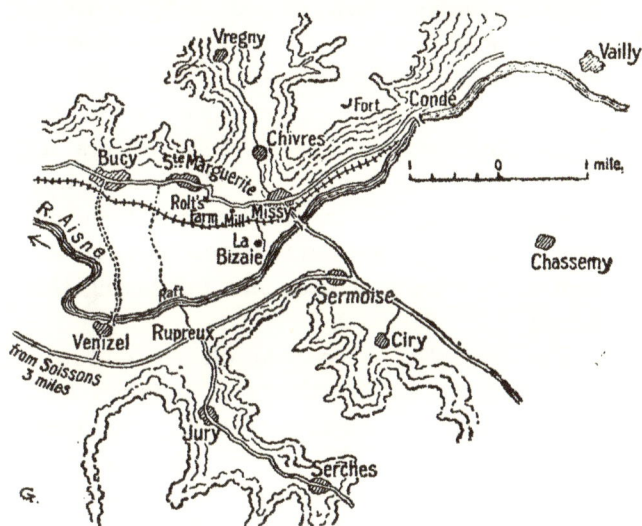

Vregny Vailly
Fort Condé
Chivres
Bucy Ste Marguerite
Rolt's
R. Aisne Farm Mill Missy
La Bizaie Chassemy
Raft Sermoise
Venizel Rupreux Ciry
from Soissons 3 miles
Jury
Serches
G.

1 mile

I was routed out again at 12.45 A.M. by Malise Graham, who had come with a message from the Divisional Commander that he wanted to see me at once at the broken bridge at Missy, a mile off through long wet grass in pitch darkness. It was

•not good "going," but we got there eventually and crossed the river, sliding down steep
slippery banks into a punt, ferried across,
and up the other side. Cuthbert eventually
turned up from somewhere, and we had
a pow-wow in the dark, resulting in fresh
orders being given for the morrow's work.

This involved new orders being written,
and it was 4 A.M. by the time we turned
in again for an hour's sleep.

A careful reconnaissance was made by
Done and some other Norfolk officers as
soon as it was light; but the result was
not promising. Fresh German trenches
had been dug commanding the open space,
and more wire had been put up during the
night.

The Norfolks were told off to lead the
assault, with the Bedfords in support and
the Cheshires in reserve. The Dorsets were
still above Sainte Marguerite, helping the
12th Brigade, and were not available.

We began by shelling that horrible
Chivres Spur, but it produced little effect,
as the Germans were in the wood and
invisible. The Norfolks pushed on, but
gradually came to a standstill in the wood,
and the day wore on with little result,

for the wood was desperately blind, and we-
were being heavily shelled at all points.

The Brigade staff sat under a hedge half-
way between La Bizaie farm and Missy;
but it was not a very happy place, for the
big shells fell nearer and nearer till we had
to make a move forward at a run for the
shelter of a big manure-heap. But even
here the Black Marias found us out, and
two of them fell within a few yards, their
explosion covering us with dirt. We were
also in view of German snipers half-way
up the hill, and bullets came thick whenever
we showed a cap or a leg beyond the muck-
heap, which, besides being distinctly unsweet,
was covered with disgusting-looking flies in
large numbers.

However, there we had to stay most of
the day. The village of Missy was inter-
mittently shelled by some huge howitzers,
and bunches of their shells blew up several
houses and nearly demolished the church,
a fine old 14th century building. A few
Norfolks were buried or killed by the falling
houses, but otherwise extraordinarily little
damage was done, and most of the shells
fell in the open, where there was nobody
worth mentioning.

At 3 P.M. I got a summons to go to Rolt
at his farm just outside Sainte Marguerite;
and a most unpleasing journey it was for
Weatherby and me. We separated, going
across the open plough and cabbage fields,
but snipers were on us the whole time, and
several times missed us by only a few inches.
We must have offered very sporting targets
to the Germans on the hill, for we ran all
the way, and—I speak for myself—we got
extremely hot.

I sprinted a good 400 yards under fire for
the shelter of a thick hedge, and when I got
there found to my disgust there was a young
river to be got over before I could reach the
cover. However, I squirmed along a fallen
bough and struggled through the fence—
to find myself face to face with Bols and
his Dorsets, whom he was bringing along
to hold the line of the fence. This gave a
certain "moral relief," and from there it
was easier going to Rolt's farm, all except
one point where the railway cut through
a hedge and crossed the stream. On this
point a German machine-gun had been laid,
and to cross it with a whole skin one had
to hurry a bit. Our Brigade machine-gun
officer, young D—— of the Bedfords, was

subsequently hit here, in the back, but not very seriously.

I concerted measures with Rolt for holding the line Missy-Sainte Marguerite, and we began to dig in places. But at 7.40 P.M. came orders for the 15th Brigade to evacuate the north bank *viâ* a new bridge near the old raft one where we had crossed; so we issued fresh orders about the 14th Brigade taking over our line, and prepared for another night march,—no sleep again.

I forgot to mention that our horses had arrived at La Bizaie early that morning, having crossed by the raft bridge the day before. Silver as usual made a desperate fuss, and was eventually knocked into the river by a mule who was crossing with him. He swam up and down the river for twenty-five minutes, refusing to come out — poor Catley in desperation all the time. But he was eventually hauled out, with my saddle and bags, of course, sopping wet. His stable shed was also shelled heavily during the day, but strange to say none of the horses or grooms were touched.

It poured in buckets that night; and as the Bedfords were streaming past the farm in the dark about 11 P.M. a terrific fire broke out from the direction of Missy, accompanied by German flarelights and searchlights. The word went round that it was a German counter-attack, and we ran out and halted the Bedfords and put them into some trenches covering the farm. But it turned out to be a false alarm; for the Germans, hearing troops moving in the dark, thought that they were going to be attacked, and opened a heavy fire on Missy, whilst the 14th Brigade and the remainder of our men still there replied to it. It eventually died down, and we resumed our march in pitch darkness and mud up to the men's knees in the water meadows by the river.

Sept. 16th.

The Cheshires came last, and we of the Brigade Staff followed them at 4 A.M. through dripping fields and criss-cross hedges, coming across the Scottish Rifles lying asleep near the pontoon bridge. They belonged to the 19th Brigade, but where the rest of the Brigade was I do not know.

On the other side of the river we found the Divisional Commander with a few of his staff. It was beastly cold and just getting light, about 5 A.M., and why Sir

Charles should be standing there I could
not at first make out. However, it turned
out that he had come down from Serches,
being somewhat anxious as to what might
be happening on the other side of the river
—with considerable justification, for if we
had been driven back on to the one bridge
which crossed the river we might have
been in a parlous state.

Half an hour later we arrived in Jury,
a tidy little village in and round which
most of the Brigade was already billeting,
and here, in a nice little house, belonging
to a worthy old couple, we took our rest,
thankful for a little peace and some sleep
at last.

And here we stayed for a week.

Not that it was all beer and skittles even
then. The 14th Brigade was still holding
Missy over the river, and there were some
serious alarms on one or two nights, necessitating troops being sent down to the river
at Rupreux, in case they were wanted.

Shells fell near Jury for a day or two,
but they gradually died away, until some
heavy guns of the 4th Division were brought
up close by and began banging away again
at the Chivres heights and beyond.   Quite

I

unnecessary we thought them, for they not
only made a hideous noise day and night,
but the enemy began searching for them
with Black Marias, some of which fell unpleasantly close to us.

It was a pretty little valley with wooded
hills, running northwards to the Aisne, and
on our right was a big plateau with huge
hay-stacks dotted about the corn-fields,
which served as excellent observing stations
for our artillery, of which by this time we
had a vast mass. The other (north) bank
of the Aisne was clearly visible from here—
in fact from the top of the biggest hay-
stack there was a regular panorama to be
seen, from the twin towers of Soissons
Cathedral on the left to the enemy's
trenches above Vailly and beyond — a
beautiful landscape typical of La Belle
France, even to the rows of poplars in the
distance, marking the Routes Nationales
from Soissons to other places of distinction.

Our business was to hold the line of the
river by digging a line of trenches from
Sermoise to near Venizel, and to cover
them with a line of outposts day and
night. This took about four companies,
and the rest were engaged in digging an-

other series of trenches on the plateau as a supporting line to the first, flanking the Jury Valley on one side and the ruins of Sermoise and Ciry on the other. This was really the first serious digging of trenches we had had during the campaign, and I remember, in the light of after experiences, how futile they must have been at the time, for they were nothing like as deep as we subsequently found to be necessary, nor had they any wire entanglements or obstacles worth mentioning. However, I expect that the French improved them greatly during the subsequent winter.

Sermoise had been desperately shelled; there were no inhabitants left, and practically every house was a heap of ruins; but though our outposts in front of it could not have been seen through the woods, the Germans continued to shell it most viciously.

On the right of Sermoise was the 13th Brigade, extended towards the 3rd Division, which had crossed the river at Vailly and was holding the slopes above it. I believe the 13th had a poor time of it, for they were scattered over open ground and in small woods which were perpetually being shelled, and they had, besides, to find a battalion or so to help the 14th Brigade in Missy.

On our left we joined hands with the 4th Division, most of whom were on the other bank, running from St Marguerite westwards; on their left were, I believe, the French, in and round Soissons.

It was a nice time for the Artillery; for guns were there in large numbers, and they had some good targets to shoot at, over Vregny and Chivres way, in the shape of the enemy's batteries and lines, when they could be seen.

The weather was mostly fine during that week, but there were two horridly cold days on which the rain came down in torrents, and did not help us in our entrenching tasks.

At last came the day which I had been expecting for some time; and I was ordered to send the Dorsets across, to begin relieving the 14th Brigade near Missy.

Sept. 24th.

They left on the 23rd, and on the 24th the Bedfords went over, preceded by the Brigade Staff at 2.30 P.M.   The Norfolks had been sent off three days before to strengthen the 3rd Division, so I had only three battalions, and of these the Cheshires were very weak. However, the K.O.Y.L.I. and West Kents (of the 13th Brigade), already holding the eastern edge of Missy, were put under my orders, besides the 15th Brigade R.F.A. under Charles Ballard (a cousin of Colin's[1]), and a Howitzer Battery (61st) of Duffus's 8th Brigade.

Weatherby and I walked across to Rolt's farm, across a series of big fields, with only an occasional bullet or shell pitching in the distance. Lord, what a poor place it was; Rolt and his staff had lived there for the last week, all lying together on straw in one or two rooms : it must have been most uncomfortable. The windows towards the north-east had been plugged up with sand-bags, so that the rooms were very dark, and the floors were deep in caked mud and dirt of all sorts. The only attraction in the main room was a big open fireplace with a huge sort of witches' cauldron standing over the hot ashes, and this was most useful in providing us with hot baths later on.

[1] Commanding the Norfolks.

Sept. 25th.

Rolt explained his position and the places which the different battalions were occupying; but beyond an occasional bombardment of Missy and losses from German snipers in trees and elsewhere, he had not suffered overmuch. However, he and his Brigade were not sorry to leave, and leave they did at 4 A.M. next morning. The awkward part of it was that one could never go out in the daytime, as the road in front of the farm leading towards Missy was under perpetual rifle-fire directly any one showed up, and several holes had been made in the farmyard gate, windows, and walls, not to mention bits of the roof taken off by shrapnel. Why they did not shell the farm more I cannot conceive. Perhaps the enemy thought it was deserted, but whilst we were there no shells fell within a couple of hundred yards of it, though some were pitched well over it, and exploded 500 yards to the rear.

I had gone to see the Dorsets and 13th Brigade in Missy on the evening before, and found them fairly well ensconced. The Dorsets were in Missy itself, with their headquarters in a really nice house with carpets and big shaded lamps, and a cellar full of excellent wine, and a nice garden all complete, and charming bedrooms—infinitely superior to our pig-sty of a farm. I seriously thought of turning them out and taking the house for the Brigade Staff, especially as our farm was not at all central but quite on the left of our line; but all our cable-lines converged on to the farm, and, in addition, the Dorset house would have been impossible to get out of for further control if Missy were shelled; so I settled to remain at the farm. The 13th Brigade—*i.e.*, K.O.Y.L.I. and West Kents, were further on, the K.O.Y.L.I. on the eastern outskirts, and the West Kents in trenches beyond them. The K.O.S.B.'s were still further south-eastwards, and reached back to the river, but there were only one or two weak companies of them.

Before dawn, and just after Rolt had left, I went to inspect the Bedfords' position, which was close to Rolt's farm, in the wood in front of it, and a beastly position it was. The wood was very damp, and when one tried to dig trenches one struck water only a foot below ground, so most of the line had to be made of breast-works. There

were German trenches within 20 yards of
our advanced trench there, and ours was
remarkably badly situated and liable to
be rushed at a moment's notice; yet it was
impossible from the lie of the ground to dig
suitable ones unless we retired altogether
for 200 yards, which of course was out of
the question. So we chanced it and stuck
it out, and luckily were never attacked
there. The men suffered there from damp
and cold, I'm afraid, for every morning a
wet and freezing fog arose in the wood,
although the weather was clear elsewhere;
but it could not be helped.

We stayed in Rolt's farm and in the
positions described for just a week. On one
day, the 27th, we had a false alarm, for
the enemy was reported as crossing the
Condé bridge at 4 A.M. in large numbers,
and everybody was at once on the *qui vive*,
the Cheshires, who were in bivouac behind
Rolt's farm, being sent back (by Sir C.
Fergusson's orders) to Rupreux, the other
side of the river. We rather doubted the
news from the start, as the Condé bridge
had, we knew, been blown up, and there
was only one girder left, by which a few

men at a time could conceivably have
crossed; but the information was so circumstantial that it sounded possible. Eventually it turned out all to be owing to the
heated imagination of a Hibernian patrol
officer of the West Kents, and we turned
in again.

Missy was shelled particularly heavily
that day from 10 to 6, and it was painful
to watch great bouquets of 8-in. H.E. shells
exploding in the village, and whole houses
coming down with a crash; it seemed as
though there must be frightfully heavy
casualties, and I trembled in anticipation
of the casualty return that night.

But the Dorsets and K.O.Y.L.I. had dug
themselves in so thoroughly in deep funk-
holes and cellars that they did not have
a single casualty; and literally the only
men wounded were three K.O.S.B.'s and
six West Kents outside the village in a
trench, who were hit by about the last
shell of the day; whilst a Bedford sniper,
an excellent shot, one Sergeant Hunt, unfortunately got a bullet through two fingers
of his right hand.

During that week it was moderately quiet,

with nothing like so many casualties as we had expected. Our supply waggons rolled up after dark right into Missy village and never lost a man, whilst the village was so thoroughly barricaded and strengthened and scientifically defended—mostly Dorset work —that we could have held out against any number. The sappers too, 17th Co. R.E., worked like Trojans under young Pottinger, a most plucky and capable youth wearing the weirdest of clothes—a short and filthy mackintosh, ragged coat and breeches, and a huge revolver.[1]

We put Rolt's farm and the mill (between that and Missy) and La Bizaie farm in a thorough state of defence, and dug hundreds of yards of trenches. In fact we should have welcomed an infantry attack, but it never came—only artillery long bowls.

In this the two howitzer batteries, especially Wilson's 61st, were splendid, and spotted and knocked out gun after gun of the enemy. He had an observing station half-way up the hill above Ste. Marguerite, to which I went occasionally, with a grand view up to Vregny and Chivres; but even

[1] I grieve very much to see that he was fatally wounded outside Ypres (15th May 1916).

here, although the O.P. was beautifully concealed, one had to be careful not to show a finger or a cap, for the German snipers in the wood below were excellent shots, and there were some narrow escapes.

The worst of it was that we could take very little exercise. I used to go out nearly every morning before sunrise to visit the posts, but was often surprised by the sun before I'd finished my rounds, and had to bolt back under fire; and after sunset I'd go round to Missy, &c., and visit the troops there. Otherwise, we could not go out at all in the daytime—it was much too "unhealthy,"—and what with numerous meals and little movement we grew disgustingly fat. I put in a lot of time drawing careful maps of the position.

The farm itself was cleaned up from roof to cellar by Moulton-Barrett and his myrmidons, but it was not perfect at first. My bed was a mass of stale blood-stains from the wounded who had lain there before we came, and St André, whose bed was not of the cleanest and exuded an odd and unpleasing smell, routed about below it, and extracted the corpse of a hen, which must have been there for ten days at least.

We cleaned up the farmyard too—it was perfectly foul when we came—but we could not show much even there, although the gate was always kept closed, for any sign of life was generally greeted with a bullet. A man got one through the knee when just outside it, and the gate itself had several holes through it. The Bedfords used to send a company at a time there for hot tea in the mornings and evenings, for they could not light fires where they were, and shivered accordingly.

Many were the schemes for improving their wood-trenches; and at last Orlebar (killed later near Wulverghem), who had been a civil engineer, drew up an arrangement for flooding the wood and retiring to a more satisfactory line. But before it could be put into practice we got orders to retire, and for the 12th Brigade on our left to relieve us.

This meant, of course, thinning the line terribly, and we were, with the 12th Brigade, somewhat nervous about it, for we did not know what it portended. But we got away during the night in perfect safety; for although there was a full moon there was also a thick mist, and the Germans never seemed to notice the movement, which required most careful staff work on the part of both Brigades.

Cuthbert, seedy, was relieved by Hickie in command of the 13th Brigade to-day.

Oct. 2nd.

By some time in the early morning of the 2nd October—1.40 A.M. it was, to be accurate —the whole Brigade had got back to Jury, and there we were told, as usual, that we were to rest and recuperate for a week; so we were not surprised at getting orders in the afternoon to move out at 6.30 P.M., our destination being a place called Droizy. I had caught a bad cold that day, due solely, I believe, to taking a "woolly" into wear for the first time; and the cold fog in which we marched did nothing to improve it. Above us was a bright clear moon, but the fog clung heavily to the valleys, and we marched in it most of the time. Desperate secrecy and quiet was observed, for we were evidently doing secret marching at night for some great object; though what it was we could only conjecture. But orders came that for the next few days we were to march at night, and during the daytime were to lie "doggo" and not show ourselves for fear of the enemy's aeroplanes.

We reached Droizy at about 11 P.M. and there found the Norfolks, who had been taken away from us at Jury ten days before and attached to the 3rd Division on our right in the direction of Vailly. Much pleased we were to see them again. They had not suffered many casualties, though they had had a stiff time at their château of Chassemy, filling the gap between the 3rd and 5th Divisions, and had been attacked several times.

The Dorsets in arriving here managed to take a wrong turn in the village and went careering off into the fog in the opposite direction to where their billets had been told off for them; but they were shortly retrieved and put on the right track. A brigade of artillery, by the way—I forget which—was attached to our brigade area that night, and distinguished itself next day by taking up a position in some open fields; which led to trouble.

Our headquarters were at a curious old castle-farm belonging to one M. Choron, right in the middle of the village, and looked after by his father, a vice-admiral, late a

director of naval construction, a nice old
fellow, who had been brutally treated by the
Germans in their retreat. There was a very
old tower to the place, no surroundings
except a farmyard, and a little old kitchen of
most antique aspect, in which we had our
meals.

Oct. 3rd.

For most of the next day we had a good
rest, and I stayed in bed to doctor my cold;
but orders soon came to move on, and the
Brigade started in the evening for Long
Pont, a village about twelve miles off,
getting there about 11. The Divisional
Commander had kindly sent a motor-car
for me; and Done, of the Norfolks (who was
also rather seedy), and Tandy, R.A., a person
of large knowledge and always interesting,
accompanied me; so we arrived at Long
Pont a long time ahead of the troops.

A great big château was gleaming in the
moonlight as we drove up, and I determined
that we should spend the night there, in
spite of the fact that the Divisional staff had
also that intention. But when I introduced
myself to the proprietor, a courteous and
frail old gentleman, the Comte de Montes-

quiou - Fezensac, he bewailed the fact that there was no room available, and this in spite of the fact that there were dozens of big windows outside, and long corridors inside, with heaps of rooms opening off them.

A visit to the village in search of a lodging revealed its true state—*i.e.*, that it was choke-full and dirty. But even then it required a good deal of persuasion before the old gentleman at last grasped the fact that I was not demanding twenty bedrooms, but only one or two empty rooms in which twenty men could lie for the night. Then he kindly produced mattresses and straw, and all was well. As for myself, he was good enough to lead me to the chamber of his late mother, a curious little room with a four-poster and locks and hasps and cupboards of Louis XIII. times, and bundles of magnificent old embroideries. As for washing apparatus—that also was almost of that date.

Next day, being Sunday, we had Divine Service in the ruins of a grand old fourteenth-century abbey which adjoined the château—wrecked in the French Revolution and again in 1830. The park also was most attractive, rather of the Trianon surroundings style; but several brigades of artillery which had to be tucked away under the trees for fear of aeroplanes rather spoilt the turf, I fear. We did, of course, as little damage as we could, and after a friendly farewell to the old couple I drove off, again in a motor, with Henvey (A.P.M. of 5th Division), and preceded the Brigade to a place called Pontdron. Here I arrived at 10 P.M.; but the Brigade, which had been heavily held up by French troops on the march, did not turn up till nearly 4 A.M.

Meanwhile I amused myself by getting the château ready. It had, of course, been occupied by Germans, and, equally of course, it had been ransacked and partly wrecked by them—though a good deal of furniture had been left. There were even candles and oil-lamps available, and of these we made full use, as well as of the bedrooms. I chose the lady's (Comtesse de Coupigny, with husband in the 21st Dragoons) bedroom. The counterpane was full of mud and sand, through some beastly German having slept on it without taking his boots off, but there was actually a satin coverlet left, and pillows. All the stud- and jewellery-cases had been opened and their contents stolen, and Madame de C.'s writing-table had also

K

been forced open, and papers and the contents of the drawers scattered on the floor.
Other unmentionable crimes had also been
committed.

Here we stayed for nearly two days,
cleaning up the château, picking up a lot of
stores in the shape of boots and caps and
clothing of all sorts—not to mention some
heavy mails from home,—and actually play-
ing lawn-tennis. At least I played with
Cadell two sets, each winning one, on a
sand court with an improvised net, and
racquets and balls somewhat the worse for
wear, with a lovely big hot bath to follow.

It was gradually borne in on us that we
were going to be moved off by train to take
part in a different theatre of the fighting
altogether; but where we should find ourselves we had not the least idea. What
caused us much joy to hear was that we
had intercepted a German wireless message,
two days after four out of the six Divisions
had left the Aisne, to say that it was "all
right, all six British Divisions were still on
the Aisne !"

Oct. 6th.

On the 6th we moved off at 2.15 P.M. and

pushed on to Béthisy St Pierre, where the Bedfords and Norfolks and ourselves halted, whilst the Dorsets and Cheshires pushed on to Verberies, so as to save time for the entraining on the morrow. We got our time-table that night, and found that we were to entrain at four stations — *i.e.,* Compiègne, Le Meux, Longueil Ste. Marie, and Pont Sainte Maxence—on the following day. Very careful arrangements and calculations had to be made, so that the whole thing should go without a hitch, and we sat up for some time at the Convent, a sort of educational establishment where Brigade Headquarters was quartered, making out the orders.

A "Brigade Area" command was allotted to me, including, besides my own Brigade, the 8th Brigade R.F.A. (howitzers), 59th Co. R.E., 15th Field Ambulance, and 4th Co. of 5th Div. Train.

Oct. 7th.

Then off at 5 A.M. next morning, ourselves for Pont Ste. Maxence. Major Vandeleur of the Scottish Rifles had just arrived to take command of the Cheshires, who had had nothing but a captain to command them since Lt.-Col. Boger was taken prisoner on the 24th August. He seemed to me a first-rate sensible fellow, but we were not destined to keep him for long.

As the Brigade was still rather short of socks, I bought as many as I could here for the men, but not many were available. It was a nice little town with a blown-up stone bridge, but the French R.E. had already constructed another of wood.

The French entraining orders are that all troops have to be at the station four blessed hours before the train starts, so as to give time to load up properly. We thus arrived at 8, and did not start till 12; but the actual entraining of the Cheshires—the only battalion with Brigade Head-quarters—took only one hour and a quarter, —not bad at all considering that there were no ramps or decent accessories, and all the vehicles had to be man-handled into the trucks.

There were two sorts of trains — one mostly for men, the other mostly for horses and vehicles; but although they were very long—thirty-four to forty cars if I remember right — they were not quite long enough for us, and several men and vehicles had to be left behind and brought on by other trains, resulting in slight incompleteness for a few days.

We rapidly reached Creil, where we were to get our final orders. What on earth would our destination be? Rumour had it that we should go to Calais, or even to Bruges; but we had no such journey after all, for we were only intended to go to Abbeville as it turned out—rather a disappointment, as we hoped it would be further afield.

Abbeville—a two hours' journey as a rule in peace time—was not reached till 8 P.M., although we were due there at 6.3 P.M. We halted by the way, for half an hour or more, at Amiens, where we made the acquaintance of a cheery crowd of "Fusiliers Marins," sturdy naval reservists from Normandy and Brittany, who covered themselves with glory later on amid the Belgian dunes.

Oct. 8th.

We were not allowed to detrain at Abbeville till 9.30 P.M., as the platforms were already occupied by other troops. It was wretchedly cold and pitch-dark by the time we had got away from the station, and we marched in dead silence through the town at 12.30 A.M. Not a soul was in the streets, not even a policeman from whom to ask the way, and we nearly lost our direction twice.

Our orders, which we received from Dunlop (5th Divisional staff), who was ensconced in a red-hot waiting-room in the goods yard, were to the effect that we were to billet near Neuilly, a village about six miles off. Done (Norfolks) had been sent ahead on the previous day to prepare the billets, but when we got near the village, after a cold march with a clear moon, Done was nowhere to be seen; and I nearly ordered the battalion to "doss down" in the road, as all the houses near were full of men of other brigades. However, Weatherby rode on, and eventually found Done in bed at the Mairie, he having been officially told that the Brigade would not be in till the following day. He had had a trying time, having been deposited by his train at a station about ten miles off, and having to make his way across country (riding) without a map and with very vague ideas of where he was to go. However, he had already told off billets for all the Brigade Area, and the troops trickled in independently by battalions and batteries, arriving by different trains and even at different stations, up to 10 A.M. in the morning. I thought it showed distinctly good work on the part of all concerned that we concentrated our "Brigade Area" so quickly and without being deficient of anything except the few vehicles which had perforce been left behind for want of trucks; but they turned up all right a day or two after.

The Brigade staff billeted at the château (as usual!), a strangely ruined-looking little place belonging to the Comte de Belleville, now at the wars. We turned up there about 4 A.M., and were guided thither by an old gardener, who thumped at the door and shouted loudly for "Madame." A woman soon appeared, and showed us most civilly to our rooms—very plain and bare but very clean. I could not quite make her out, for though she was dressed in the plainest of print clothes she did not talk like a servant —in fact she talked like a lady; so I put her down as some relation perhaps who was helping Mme. de Belleville. But later in the morning I discovered that she was Madame la Comtesse herself, who had kindly risen at that unearthly hour to let us in, and that there were no servants in the establishment at all except the old gardener and a nurse.

Our movements were still by way of being kept a dead secret, so we went off in the afternoon at 6 P.M., reinforced now by some divisional cavalry and divisional cyclists. The road, in the dark, was an extremely complicated one, as it involved about twenty turnings and movement along narrow lanes with high hedges and big trees, making it quite impossible to see for more than a few yards. So I took the guiding of the column into my own hands, and distributed the rest of my staff along it to see that the different units did not miss the way and kept well closed up. The result was good, and after 5 hours march, *viâ* Agenvilliers and Gue- schard, we reached the little village of Boufflers about 11 P.M. Here, at an odd little Nouvel Art "Château" — or rather small country house, empty of its owners— belonging to M. Sagebien, Préfet de Niort, we of the Brigade staff put up, the rest of the command being billeted in the tiny villages lining each bank of the tiny stream near—I have forgotten its name.

Oct. 9th.

It was a nice sunny day on the morrow, and we got our orders by midday that we were to move off at 2 P.M. We wrote out Brigade orders and prepared to start, when suddenly post-haste came some orders cancelling these, and telling us that we were to drop our transport and be moved off at once in a series of motor-buses to a place called Diéval.

And then began a lovely jumble, which resulted (not our own fault) in getting to Diéval rather later than we should have done had we trusted to our own unaided powers of locomotion.

We moved off at 2 P.M., only taking blanket-waggons which were to dump blankets and supplies into the buses. These were to have turned up on the Haravesnes-Fillièvres road at 7 P.M.; in any case it would have been a complicated job getting into them in the dark, but they did not arrive till midnight, owing to some mechanical breakdowns in the column. The first lot of "camions" were to have taken six battalions—*i.e.*, the 14th Brigade, which was just ahead of us, and half of the 15th Brigade. But when they did arrive, there were only enough for three and three-quarter battalions; so we bivouacked in more or less peace by the roadside until this bunch had moved off and returned from Diéval to fetch us. Horribly cold it was too, and we only kept moderately warm by pulling down several straw stacks — which we carefully put together again next day—and covering ourselves up in the straw.

I had, by the way, an extremely narrow escape from being killed that night. I had been lying down just off the road, when it struck me that I should find out more of what was happening and going to happen if I went to the head of the camion column and interviewed the officer in charge. It was a tramp of a mile or more through the 14th Brigade, and I found out something of what I wanted; but when I returned to the bivouac I heard that, not two minutes after I had started, a motor-bus had swerved off the road and passed exactly over the place where my head had been. It very nearly went over St André and Moulton-Barrett, who were lying a few feet away, as it was. Of course the driver could not see any one lying down in the dark.

Oct. 10*th.*

Next morning we had breakfast at 7.30
in the field, and still the buses had not
returned. We waited in that place till
11 o'clock before they turned up, and then
clambered into them as quickly as we
could—twenty-two men to a bus, sixteen
buses to 300 metres being the allowance.
Even then we had to leave about two
battalions behind for a third trip.

I got into the first bus—a very fast one,
—and reached Diéval some time before the
rest of the Brigade; but there was no room
in the town for another Brigade, as it was
already full of the 14th.

I went to see Rolt, and got into telephone
communication with Divisional Headquarters
on the subject, and they gave me leave to
billet at La Thieuloye, one and a half miles
back and off the road. So W. and I walked
back and turned the buses off there just
as they were arriving.

A curious sight were the hundreds, or
even thousands, of French civilians whom
we met—all men of military age, whom the
French Army was sending away westwards
out of Lille; for it was likely that Lille
would shortly be invested by the Germans,

and they did not want this large batch of
recruits and reservists to be interned in
Germany.

The rest of the Brigade—transport, horses,
and all—rolled up by 6 P.M., the horses being
very tired after their long night march.

From what I could gather German cavalry
was trying to get round our north-west flank,
whilst a big fight was going on at Arras.
Lille, with a few Territorial battalions in
it, was still holding out, but was surrounded
by the enemy. Hence the hurry. But we
ought to have plenty of troops now to keep
the Germans off. It was very puzzling to
make out what was happening, for we had
not even the vaguest idea where the rest
of our own Army was, let alone the French
or Germans. Nobody seemed to know anything, except that we should probably soon
be fighting again.

Our quarters that night were a horrid
little château—empty, damp, and desolate,
in a deserted wilderness of a place, with no
furniture except some straw, a mattress or
two, and some packing-cases. So here we
tried to make ourselves comfortable, and
succeeded in lighting a fire and settling
down. But it was beastly cold and damp.

Oct. 11*th.*

We marched at 7.20 A.M. in a thick damp mist, myself being in charge of the right column of the Division, consisting of the Brigade, the 15th Brigade R.F.A., 108th heavy battery (under Tyrrell, late Military Attaché at Constantinople), 17th R.E. Fd. Co., and cyclists (who, by the way, did not turn up, having been sent ahead). On the way to Béthune we were evidently coming into touch with the enemy, for I received orders to detach two companies (Cheshires) to our right flank at Fonquières‒Verquin to support the French. But they returned in the course of the afternoon, not being wanted.

Outside Béthune we halted for some time, and were regaled with soup and pears by some hospitable ladies at luncheon - time. And then we received orders to push through the town and cover it along the bend of the canal and across the arc of it (from Essars due east) with three battalions, the Norfolks being sent away to the east to help the French about Annequin.

It was perfectly flat country and difficult to defend, as it was so cut up by high hedges and suburbs; but I went round it in the

afternoon, inspected it carefully, and posted
the battalions.   Towards evening, however,
we had orders to fall back into the town
—the French taking over the outposts—and
billet there, our Headquarters being in the
Grande Place—a large square with a curious
old belfry in the middle — at a wine-shop,
No. 34.   Here we were well looked after,
and had each of us a lovely hot bath, provided by a marvellous system of gas-jets
which heated the water in about five minutes.

Oct. 12th.

Off eastwards next morning at 8.30 A.M.
through a freezing thick fog—so thick that
one could not see twenty yards in front of
one.   The big open space in the town
through which we passed was occupied
with masses of Spahis, Moorish troops, and
Algerians of all sorts, looking miserably cold
in their scarlet jackets and white burnouses.
The idea was that we were to push forward
to Festubert and act as a pivot, with our
right near the canal at Rue de l'Épinette,
to the 3rd Division and the remainder of
the Corps, which were swinging slowly
round to their right so as eventually to
face south-east and take La Bassée.

At first my orders directed me to leave a gap between myself and the canal, the gap being filled by French troops; but shortly afterwards I was told that the Brigade was to hold from Festubert to the canal, relieving the French cavalry here, who were to hold on till we got there; and I paid a visit to the French cavalry General at Gorre to make sure that this would be done. The line was a horribly extended one—about two miles; and the prospect was not entrancing. However, I detached the Dorsets to move along the canal bank from Gorre and get touch with the French. Very glad I was that I had done so, for they had severe fighting there that day against a strong force of the enemy, who tried to get in between us and the French.

The Bedfords I ordered to hold Givenchy. The first rumour was that the French had evacuated Givenchy before we could come up, and that the Germans had occupied it; but this turned out not to be true after all. The Cheshires held Festubert, and the Norfolks were in Divisional reserve somewhere in rear.

Meanwhile the Germans were attacking

along the canal; but the Dorsets checked
them most gallantly, losing poor Roper,
killed in leading a charge, and a number
of men. Lilly was wounded at the same
time.

The Headquarters passed most of that day
—and an extremely busy Staff day it was
—in a little pot-house in Festubert, and we
slept in a tiny house put at our disposal
by one Masse, gendarme, a gallant old
soldier, who was the only representative
of civilian authority in the place, the
Maire having bolted, and his second in
command being sick unto death in his own
house.

Oct. 13th.

The night went off fairly peaceably, but
early next morning we had a nasty jar,
for it was reported at 8 A.M. that Majors
Vandeleur (commanding) and Young (2nd
in command) of the Cheshires, together
with a company and a half, had all been
made prisoners or killed by the Germans
about Rue d'Ouvert. The circumstantial
story was that the early morning patrols
had reported that Rue d'Ouvert (about a
mile in front of Festubert) was free of

Germans; that Vandeleur and Young had gone out with two platoons to make sure of it, had got into Rue d'Ouvert and found it empty at first, but had been subsequently fired at from the houses, surrounded by superior numbers, and had been taken prisoners after losing half their men. As for Shore's company, who were supporting them, they had disappeared completely and had apparently suffered the same fate.

I immediately sent out scouts to find out the truth; but a very heavy fire was by this time opened on the remainder of the Cheshires, and the scouts could not get through. No further news even came in of Shore's company, but we could not believe that it had really been scuppered, or else there would have been much more firing, and we must have had some news of the disaster, if it had occurred.

And so it was. Towards 3 o'clock we had news that the company was safely tucked away in some ditches, holding its front, and had had practically no losses, although it could not move out without attracting a heavy artillery fire.

Not till long afterwards did I hear what had really happened to Vandeleur, and then

it was from his own lips in January 1915,
he having escaped from Crefeld just before
Christmas. It appeared that he and Young
had gone up with about half a company in
support of some scouts who had reported Rue
d'Ouvert clear. The half company did not,
however, go into Rue d'Ouvert, for they
were violently attacked by superior forces
before they got there. They lost heavily,
but succeeded in getting into a farmhouse,
which they held all day against the enemy,
hoping that we should move out and rescue
them. But we, of course, had been told
circumstantially that they were already
prisoners at 8 A.M., so knew nothing of it
and took no action.

The enemy set the house on fire, and the
gallant little garrison put it out with wine
from the cellars, for they were cut off
from the water-supply. Their numbers
were reduced to about thirty, when they
were again attacked in overwhelming force
at 9 P.M., and many of the remainder
(including Vandeleur) wounded. Then there
was no choice, and they surrendered, being
complimented on their gallantry by the
German General in command at La Bassée.
They were then sent off to Germany *viâ*

Douai, and were most abominably treated
on the journey, wounded and all being
pigged together in a filthy cattle-truck three
inches deep in manure for thirty hours without food or water, insulted and kicked by
the German escort and a brute of a lieutenant at Douai, and finally sent to Crefeld,
where they were again ill-treated, starved,
and left in tents with no covering — their
greatcoats, and even their tunics, having
been taken away,—nothing to lie on except
damp and verminous straw, on muddy wet
ground. Many men died of this treatment.
The officers were treated somewhat better,
but very harshly, and were never given
enough to eat. Vandeleur's escape is "another story."

That day was a terrible day: Givenchy
was bombarded heavily by the Germans
for hours, and rendered absolutely unten-
able. The Bedfords held out there gallantly,
and stuck to one end of the village whilst
the enemy was in possession of the other;
but the heavy artillery was too much for
them, and after losing about sixty casualties, many of them killed by falling houses,
they gradually fell back to trenches in rear
of the village. Griffith (commanding) and

Macready (Adjutant) came to see me about 3 P.M., their clothes and faces a mass of white dust and plaster, and explained the situation; but there was nothing to be done, as we had no reserves, and had to stick it out as best we could.

But by far the worst was what happened to the Dorsets. The account of what happened was rather confused, but it appears that, depending on their left being supported by the Bedfords at Givenchy, and their right by the K.O.S.B.'s (13th Brigade) on the south side of the Canal, they pushed forward for some distance and dug themselves roughly in, after driving the Germans back. Then suddenly their front trench was attacked from the left rear, and a heavy fire poured upon their men as they retired on their supports. They were also shot down from the embankment on the south of the Canal—from just where they had expected the K.O.S.B.'s to be.

At one place about twenty Germans advanced and held up their hands. The Dorsets then advanced to take their surrender, when suddenly the twenty fell down flat, and about 100 more who had come close up under cover of the incident opened

a heavy fire on our men and killed a lot.
The battalion retired slowly, in admirable
order, to Pont Fixe and the trenches covering it, and put a big factory there in a
state of defence.   But they had lost very
heavily: thirteen officers killed (including
Pitt   and   Davidson),   wounded   (including
Bols and Rathbone), and missing; and 112
men killed and wounded, and 284 missing—
most of these, I fear, being killed, for
numbers of bodies were discovered later
on between the lines.   Bols was at first
reported killed, but he only had a bullet
through his back, narrowly missing the
spine, and another through his arm.   He
fell unseen and had to be left behind when
the battalion retired, and was found and
stripped of all his kit by the Germans; but
he recovered in the darkness, and managed
to scramble and crawl back to the English
lines.   (From here he was sent to London,
arriving there only two days later.)

We also lost two guns there, which had
been brought up from the 15th R.F.A.
Brigade and could not be got away in time.
A gallant attempt was made by volunteers
to recover them next day, but it was useless and only cost more lives.

The Dorsets as well as the Bedfords also lost one of their machine-guns. Altogether it was a damnable day, and we on the staff were also pretty well exhausted by the amount of staff work and telegrams and messages going through all day. The 2nd Devons (or rather two companies of them) were sent to the assistance of the Dorsets in the evening; but it was a difficult thing to carry out, as the banks of the Canal, along which they had to go, were soft and boggy, and they had much difficulty in getting their S.A.A. carts along.

The Brigade Headquarters withdrew in the evening from Festubert to a foul big farm about half a mile back. This, from a particularly offensive big cesspool in the middle of the yard, we labelled Stink Farm (it had 1897 in big red tiles on the roof). It was a beastly place, and W. and I had to sleep in a tiny room on a couple of beds which had not seen clean mattresses or coverings. for certainly ten years or more. There were, however, plenty of barns and clean straw for the men.

Oct. 14th.

The general idea was to continue to push

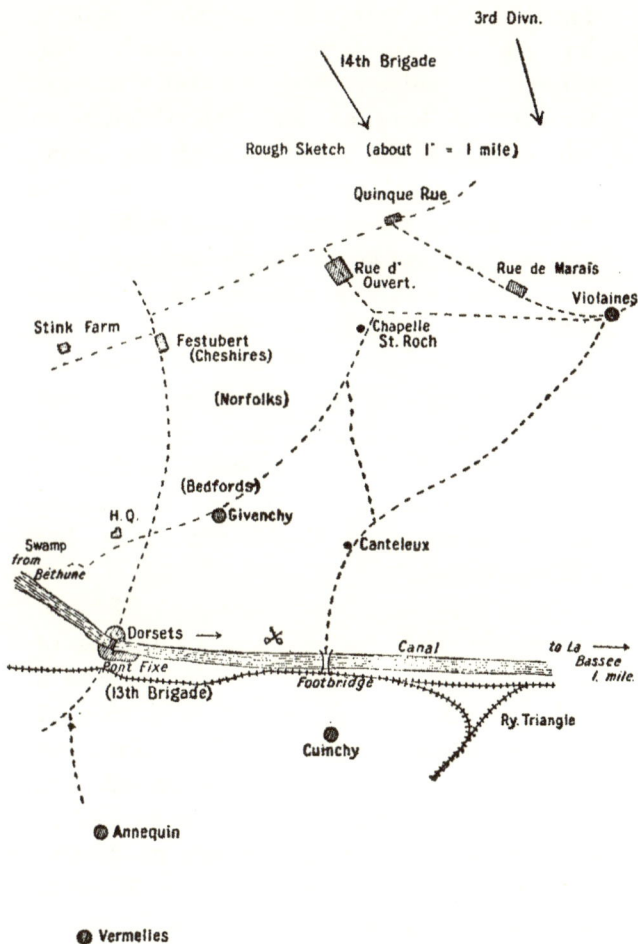

forward, with our right on the Canal, to let the 3rd Division swing round. But though we did our best, we could not get forward as long as the 13th Brigade on our right, on the other side of the Canal, were held up — for if we advanced that would merely mean getting our right flank exposed and enfiladed by the enemy.

Two more companies of the Devons arrived, to support the remains of the Dorsets, from the 14th Brigade, the battalion being under Lieutenant - Colonel Gloster. But we could not do any good, and except for an immense number of messages we did little all day. The enemy was in some strength in our front, but did not attack.

There was very heavy firing at 6.30 P.M. and again at 9 P.M. all along our line of outposts, and we thought at first it was a night attack; but it was only a case of false alarm on the part of the Dorsets on the right and the 14th Brigade on our left.

I forgot to mention that we were told to advance with the 13th Brigade at 3 P.M., but the latter were held up, and relieved in the evening by the 58th French Brigade. What immediately happened to the 13th I do not remember; but they were eventually sent round on to the left of the 14th Brigade, I believe.

Oct. 15th.

The French were meanwhile heavily attacking Vermelles, and we were to be ready to advance alongside them if they succeeded. I sent Moulton-Barrett to the Canal to receive the message from the French through Chapman (our Divisional Intelligence officer) when it came. But it never came, for the French made no progress; so we did nothing except dig proper trenches and strengthen our positions.

In the evening came in reports that the Germans were withdrawing and evacuating posts in our front. The remains of the Dorsets were withdrawn into reserve, and the Devons came under my orders in their place.

Oct. 16th.

There was a dripping thick mist nearly all day, and we pushed on under its cover— the Bedfords into Givenchy (losing poor Rendall, killed by the retiring Germans), and the Norfolks into Rue d'Ouvert and St

Roch, whilst the Devons, ordered to make the footbridge to Canteleux road "good," pushed on in the afternoon. But it got so absolutely pitch-dark that it was impossible to make a cohesive advance; so after getting close to the footbridge and coming under a heavy fire thence, the Devons fell back again, all the more justified since Canteleux was reported still occupied by the enemy on their left flank. A vast amount of staff work all day. We returned to the Festubert pothouse in the evening.

Oct. 17th.

The first question was, Was Canteleux occupied by the enemy? Preparations were made to shell it at 6 A.M., but figures were seen strolling about there which did not look very German. Shortly afterwards the Norfolks reported that they had about sixty men in it who had penetrated thither during the night. The Bedfords at first were still convinced that the men in Canteleux were German, but we disabused them as soon as we heard the truth for certain, and for a change shelled some farms to our front whence hostile machine-gun fire was proceeding, setting one on fire.

In the afternoon we were ordered to advance to the line: bridge—Canteleux—Violaines; and again the Devons pushed on, slowly, in connection with the French, but were again obliged to retire from the vicinity of the bridge by heavy fire, and took up their position in the advanced position that the Dorsets had occupied on the 13th.

The Cheshires, under the three gallant captains, Shore, Mahony, and Rich, meanwhile worked well forward and reported their arrival at Violaines at 4 P.M., having reached it *viâ* Rue du Marais.

A desperate amount of work again, 5 A.M. to 11 P.M. I only got out of the pothouse for twenty minutes all day, and that was at 5 P.M.

Thus we had pushed forward some way on our line by the evening, and the 14th Brigade was in touch with the Cheshires and moving slowly forward—but very slowly.

Oct. 18th.

Next day the usual "general advance" was ordered for 6 A.M., and the artillery loosed off a lot of shells on to where we thought the enemy were. But it was really quite useless our advancing on the right unless the French did also, for the Germans held the south bank of the Canal in front of the latter, and any advance by us merely exposed our right flank to a terrible enfilade fire. .

Major-General Morland, who had succeeded Sir C. Fergusson in command of the Division, now turned up, and to him I explained these things.   The Railway Triangle was the worst place, for it was heavily held by Germans, who had dug themselves in behind stockades of rails and trucks and defied even our howitzers; but it was difficult, very difficult, for the latter to make good practice at them here, as the country was so flat, yet so cut up with high trees and fences that it was almost impossible to get an observing station or to see what one was firing at.

I shifted Brigade Headquarters about 1 P.M. to a nice little house with garden, close behind the cross-roads half a mile west of Givenchy, and here we stayed for four un-pleasant days. We had to be very careful, after dark, not to show a light of any sort towards the enemy, and had to plaster up the windows with blankets and things which every now and then came down with a run, causing rapid transition to total darkness and discomfort. But it was a good little place on the whole, and quite decently furnished.

In the afternoon I went to observe what I could from Givenchy. The village was already in ruins, with most of the church blown down, whilst the only place to observe from was from between the rafters of a barn on the eastern outskirts—most of the roof having been carried away by shrapnel. There was not much to see; for although Givenchy stood on the only little rise in the country, a tree in one direction and a chapel in the other blocked most of the view towards La Bassée. In front of us lay the Bedford trenches, with the Devons on their right and the French on their right again. One could just see the farm buildings of Canteleux, and the spires of part of La Bassée, but St Roch was invisible, and so were the Norfolk trenches.

Later on I went to interview Gloster, commanding the Devons; but I did not find him. With a French orderly and a Devon officer I rode through Pont Fixe and turned to the left along the Canal. Then we had to dismount at a bend of the Canal, which brought us into view of the enemy, and we bolted across bullet-swept ground into the right of the Devon trenches. Here I waited about an hour; but Gloster did not turn up, and meanwhile a heavy hostile fusilade went on which effectually prevented my putting my nose above ground. I don't know whether they had spotted me going into that trench, but I do know the parapet received an unfair share of bullets.

When it was nearly dark I cleared out and went to the Canal and whistled for my mare (I had been riding Squeaky). The French orderly turned up leading her, but his own horse had gone,—as he ruefully explained, "à cause d'un obus qui a éclaté tout près dans l'eau." He was a good youth: he had stuck to my mare and let his own go, as he could not manage both. However, virtue was rewarded, and he found his horse peacefully grazing in the outskirts of Pont Fixe.

When I reached Headquarters I found Gloster there, for he had come to look for me; so I had the required interview with him and settled about a rearrangement of his trenches.

Oct. 19th.

We actually had a quiet night—six and a half hours' sleep without being disturbed at all.

An attack was ordered for 7 A.M. in conjunction with the French. But the French were not ready at that hour. I was told that the 6th battalion of the 295th Regiment,

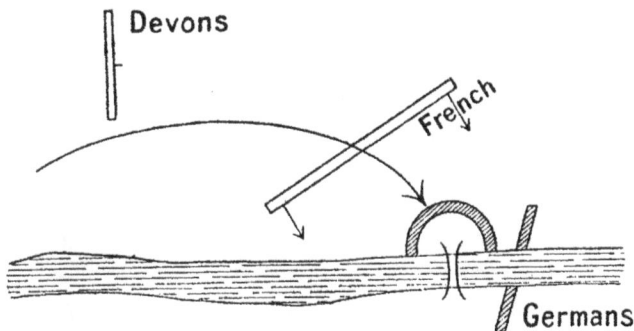

which had now been brought over to the north of the Canal, was to be under my orders; but hardly had I heard this when I received a message at 9.25 A.M. that the French were going to attack at 9.30. At noon they did so, and very pluckily. It was, however, impossible to assist them, for they (the 6/295) ran forward and attacked the Canal and footbridge obliquely, completely

masking any action possible by the Devons.
They lost heavily, I fear, but it really was
not our fault, though at one time they
seemed to think it was.

I went to talk to Lieut.-Col. Perron, who
commanded the detachment (6/295 and a
few Chasseurs à Cheval), in the afternoon;
but the interview did not enlighten me very
much. The commander of the 6/295, however, one Baron d'Oullenbourg, was most
intelligent, and a gallant fellow with plenty
of *nous*. He was badly wounded two days
afterwards in another attempt.

I was so much struck with the plucky
way in which the 6/295 pushed on under
heavy fire that I sent a complimentary note
both to the battalion and to General Joubert,
commanding the 58th Brigade on the other
side of the Canal—for the battalion belonged
(to start with) to his brigade. They published both my notes in the *Ordre du Jour*
of the Division, and d'Oullenbourg received
a Légion d'Honneur in consequence (so St
André told me). Anyway, he thoroughly
deserved it.

Meanwhile we heard that the Cheshires,
Manchesters, and K.O.S.B.'s were all held
up near Violaines by a beastly sugar factory

which the Germans occupied on the road
north of La Bassée, and they could not get
on at all.

Generals Morland and Franklin turned
up in the afternoon. We were perpetually
being urged to advance and attack, but
how could we? There was nothing to
attack in front of us except La Bassée, a
couple of miles off, and we could not advance
a yard in that direction without exposing
our right flank to a deadly enfilade fire from
across the Canal, for the Germans were
still strongly holding that infernal railway
triangle, and nothing availed to get them
out of it.[1] General Morland wisely, therefore, ordered me not to advance in force.

Later on we heard that the Cheshires had
made a gain of 800 yards, but had got
so extended that they asked for a Bedford company to support them, and this
I sent.

In the evening I went to examine a
French 75 mm. battery, and had the whole
thing explained to me. The gun is simply
marvellous, slides horizontally on its own
axle, never budges however much it fires,

[1] They are still there (August 1917)!

M

and has all sorts of patent dodges besides:
but it is no use painting the lily!

Wilson, of the 61st Howitzers, was, by
the way, a little aggrieved by this French
battery coming and taking up its position
close alongside him and invading his observing stations. The captain also got on his
nerves, for he was somewhat excitable, and
his shells were numerous that burst pre-
maturely, whilst a house only 100 yards
off, which should have been well under the
trajectory of his shells, was several times
hit by them. However, he doubtless caused
much damage to the enemy.

On the 20th and 21st the Germans kept
us fairly busy with threatened attacks, especially on the Cheshires at Violaines; but nothing definite happened, although we were
kept on the perpetual *qui vive*, and could
not relieve our feelings by attacking, for we
had orders to "consolidate our position."

By this time we occupied a line as
follows :—

 Canal from crossed swords (*v.* map) to
  300 yards North (French).
 Thence to Canteleux (excl.) (Devons).
 Canteleux to Pt. 21 [1] (Norfolks).

   [1] Nearly half-way to Violaines.

Pt. 21 to Violaines (Do. patrols).

Violaines (Cheshires and one company Bedfords).

Givenchy, in reserve (three companies Bedfords).

On the evening of the 21st there was serious news on our left. Although the Cheshires were still in occupation of Violaines, it looked as if they might have to retire from it very soon, as the right of the 14th Brigade, on the Cheshires' left, was being driven back. Violaines, however, was very important, and to let the Germans get a footing here was most dangerous. So, with General Morland's sanction, and after communicating with the Cheshires, who cheerily said they could hold out all right, I told the Cheshires to stick to Violaines, throwing their left flank back in case the line to their left was penetrated.

Oct. 22nd.

A very anxious day ensued. At 6 A.M. the Cheshires were invaded in front and flank by a surprise attack of the enemy in great force, and had to fall back towards Rue du Marais, losing heavily. Some Dorsets (who had been for the last three days at Stink Farm and were sent as a support to the 13th Brigade) were supporting them, but they could not do much, and they also lost a number of men. From what I could gather, the Cheshires had been digging in the dark round the southern and eastern flank of the village, and had their sentries out, but apparently not quite far enough out for such thick weather, and when the Germans appeared rushing through the fog they were taken at a disadvantage, for they had cast their equipment in order to dig, and the covering party was quickly cut down.

This, at all events, was what I made out from the surviving officers, of whom one, 2nd Lieut. Pogson, was the senior. Mahony and Rich, fighting gallantly, had been killed, and Shore wounded and taken prisoner. About 200 men were also killed and wounded out of about 600, and a good many of the Bedfords with them, including poor Coventry (late Transport officer) killed.

At 8.30 A.M. I was ordered to send my three companies of Bedfords from Givenchy to St Roch, to support the 13th Brigade, who were hanging on about Rue du Marais. But, besides thus depriving me of my only reserve, these companies had great difficulty in getting to their places, as the country over which they had to pass was heavily shelled by the enemy, and they took a long time getting there.

I heard that the combined 13th and 14th Brigades were to make a counter-attack on Rue du Marais in the afternoon, and this was certainly attempted. But owing to the mix-up of their battalions in the enclosed country it was impossible to arrange a combined movement under the heavy fire, and it was eventually given up — merely confused fighting taking place during the afternoon. It was, however, sufficient to stop the Germans for the time being. One reason for the difficulty — as I afterwards heard — was that the officer temporarily commanding the 13th Brigade had, by some mischance, got stuck right in the firing line with his staff and signal section, and could not be got at, nor could he move himself or issue orders,—a useful though unhappy warning to Brigadiers.

I moved with the Brigade Staff from my house at Givenchy to another house about 600 yards west of Festubert, so as to be more behind the centre of my Brigade.

During the night, in pursuance of orders

from the Division, we fell back on to a
somewhat undefined line of defence covering
the front of Festubert - Givenchy, and proceeded to dig ourselves in along a line
entirely in the open fields, and very visible,
I fear, to the enemy. Some battalions could
not get sufficient tools, and were not half
dug in by daylight. However, the Germans
must have suffered considerably themselves,
for they did not attack us in the morning,
although their Field Artillery kept up a
heavy shrapnel fire. The West Ridings
(13th Brigade) were put under my orders.

Oct. 23rd.

We were shelled all the morning, but had
no serious casualties.

My Brigade now consisted of the Devons
(14th Brigade), West Ridings (13th Brigade),
and the Norfolks (15th Brigade). The
remains of the Cheshires and Dorsets were
withdrawn and put into the Rue de Béthune
hamlet in rear of Festubert, under orders
of the 13th Brigade as their reserve, whilst
the Bedfords were attached to, I think, the
14th Brigade, somewhere Quinque Rue way.
It was a glorious jumble, and what happened
to the rest of the 13th Brigade I do not

know. I believe they combined in some way with the 14th, but I know that two days afterwards the Brigadier was left with only one fighting battalion, the West Kents, I think.

However, my command was shortly increased considerably by the arrival of Commandant Blanchard with the 2nd Battalion of the 70th Infanterie de Ligne (Regulars). Blanchard was a good solid man, and I put him to hold Givenchy in conjunction with the Devons, who were now occupying the Bedford trenches there. The French on the right of the 70th gave us acute reason for anxiety by retiring calmly from their trenches when they were shelled; but it was only their way, for half an hour afterwards they trotted back into them quite happily, much to the relief of the Devons and their exposed flank.

I rode down to Givenchy in the afternoon to see Blanchard and make arrangements for holding the village, and here I met Williams (now commanding the Devons since his C.O., Gloster, had been hit two days before, not very seriously) and talked matters over with him.

We expected a night attack, and were

certainly not in a strong position to resist
it. Had we been driven in we should have
been jammed into the swamp in rear,
between the Canal and the Gorre-Festubert
road, which would have been extremely
unpleasant. So I issued orders to hold tight
at all costs, besides secret orders to certain
C.O.'s as to what they were to do if we
were badly mauled and had to fall back.

Luckily no attack took place, and we had
a fairly quiet night.

Oct. 24th.

At 7 A.M. I received the encouraging news
(from the 2nd corps) that we were going
to be heavily attacked to-day, and what
certainly gave colour to it was the arrival
of a large number of Black Marias during
breakfast, which exploded within an unpleasantly narrow radius of our house. It
is quite conceivable that the position of
our Headquarters had been given away
by some spy. Anyhow, it looked like it,
and we decamped at 9.30 to a cottage half
a mile back. Perhaps it is as well that we
did so, for at 9.40 a big shell arrived through
the roof and exploded in my late bedroom,
tearing out the corner of the house wall

and wrecking the stable; whilst nearly at the same moment another shell completely wrecked the house just opposite, where Ballard (commanding 15th Brigade R.F.A.) had been spending the night. He also had cleared out about an hour before.

Before I went I sent my senior officer, Ballard (Norfolks), down to Givenchy to take local command over the French and English troops there, and am glad I did so, for it introduced unity of command and satisfaction. The Devons down there were meanwhile getting exhausted after their long spell in the trenches; but I had no troops to relieve them with, nor any reserve.

The "attack" did not materialize, and we had a fairly quiet afternoon, the Germans limiting their activities to digging themselves in and sniping perpetually.

It was an extraordinarily warm day, and we sat in the cottage with windows and doors wide open till long after dark. An attack was made about 10 P.M. on the French the other side of the Canal, but it was too far off to interest us much.

Oct. 25th.
Another lovely warm day of Indian

summer. Also of many shells, some falling pretty close to our cottage. The Germans were seen making splendid use of the folds in the ground for driving saps and connecting up their heads into trenches getting nearer and nearer to our lines. And we could do nothing but shell them and snipe them as best we could, but with little result, for artillery observation-posts were almost impossible, and snap-shooting at an occasional head or shovel appearing above ground produced but small results.

Three French batteries arrived during the morning and were put under Blanchard's orders in the swampy wood behind Givenchy. Some spasmodic attacks occurred on the trenches east of the village, and the French lost rather heavily; for the Germans got into some of their evacuated trenches and killed the wounded there. A speedy counter-attack, however, drove them out again. The Devons lost two officers (Besley and Quick) and ten men killed and thirty-eight wounded.

At 4.50 P.M. I got a message saying large columns of the enemy had been seen by the French issuing from La Bassée and Violaines, and I was ordered peremptorily to be ready to counter-attack at once, with my whole force if required.

Sir Horace Smith-Dorrien arrived alone an hour or so afterwards, and I pointed out our situation to him; he entirely concurred in my view, and heartened me up considerably by quite recognising the state of affairs and congratulating us, and especially the Devons, on sticking it out so well.

Maynard (Major in the Devons) arrived about midnight and took over command of the battalion, he having been on the staff of the 2nd Corps.

Oct. 26th.

Next morning I rode out again to Givenchy to see Ballard and my fresh French troops; for the 6/285th (Captain Gigot), the 5/296th (Commandant Ferracci—a typical little Corsican and a good soldier), and a squadron of Chasseurs à Cheval had arrived to strengthen us, besides the three batteries aforesaid (under Commandant Menuan). The 2/70th (now under Captain de Ferron) and the 6/295th (lately under Baron d'Oullenbourg, now wounded; I have, I fear, forgotten his successor's name) were, of course, also under me; so I had a nice little com-

mand now of three English and four French
battalions, four English and three French
batteries, and a French squadron. St André
as liaison officer was of the greatest possible
use to me, being both tactful and suggestive
as to dealing with my new command, and
keeping up splendid communication.

I then relieved the Devons by the 6/295th
—and well they deserved it after their bad
time for the last week,—and put the 296th
in reserve at various points during the
night, sending the Devons as reserve to
the Norfolks and West Ridings at Les
Plantins, between Givenchy and Festubert.

There was practically no shelling at all
during the whole day—I wonder why; nor
did the enemy make any movement. But
we heard of their bringing big guns on to
the rising ground at Billy and Haisnes, to
the south of La Bassée, and tried to "find"
them with our howitzers and heavy artillery battery.

Oct. 27th.

The reliefs were not finished till 2.30 A.M.
—largely owing to some idiots, French or
English, loosing off their rifles as they left
the trench, which brought a heavy fire on us

from the enemy and delayed matters for a long time. It was also not easy—although we had made elaborate and detailed arrangements—to relieve British by French troops in pitch darkness, for, interpreters being scarce, they could not understand each other when they met.

We heard that there was an attack on the 14th Brigade on our left about 1 A.M., and that 200 Germans had got in behind the K.O.Y.L.I. and were still there; what happened to them I do not know. The 7th Brigade, on the left of the 14th, had also been driven in, and the 14th Brigade received orders to make a counter-attack in the evening, with the Devons held ready to help them if required.

During the day one Captain Pigeonne and his batch of gendarmerie arrived, with orders to clear Festubert of its civilian inhabitants. This was necessary, as the Germans were pretty close up to it and there were undoubtedly spies, and even snipers were reported in and about the village. But hardly any people were found except the lunatic inhabitants of a small asylum, together with their staff, who had stayed there, both men and women, most devotedly for the last week, with practically nothing to eat in the whole place. The inhabitants were ordered to clear out, and some of them did. But others hid, and yet others crept back again by night, so the result was practically *nil*. One poor old woman was hunted out three times, but she returned yet once more, piteously saying that she had nowhere to go to, and wanted to die in her own house.

During the evening General Joubert, commanding the 58th Brigade, arrived with orders to take over command of all French troops north of the Canal. So my international command had not lasted long. But they sent me a liaison N.C.O. of their artillery — a most intelligent man with a yellow beard—and I was still allowed to call on the French batteries for assistance whenever I needed them.

Oct. 28th.

Joubert was a typical French General, white-moustached, short, courteous, gallant, and altogether charming and practical, and I went again to see and consult him next morning at Givenchy, cantering through the swampy woods at the back, where most

of our seven batteries were posted under
excellent cover. I also, before going to bid
him adieu, had written him what I thought
was a charming letter, congratulating him
on the "galanterie de ses troupes." Alas,
St André was out when I wrote the letter,
or probably I should have expressed it
differently; I hear it was subsequently
published in orders, but I trust it was
edited first!

The night had been extraordinarily quiet,
and after my visit to Joubert the situation
was so peaceful that I walked back a bit
to inspect a third line of trenches that
were being dug by civilians and spare
troops under R.E. supervision. I was not
much edified at the portion that the 15th
Brigade had been told off to, for it was
within 150 yards of a bunch of houses in
front, under cover of which the Germans
could have come up quite close; and if
they had put a selection of their snipers
into them, we should have had a poor time.
But I quite allow that I was at a loss,
owing to the awkward ground, to suggest
anything better. We had also a mile of
front to cover, with three weak battalions
and a difficult line, whilst the four French

battalions had been allotted altogether only half a mile of excellent natural trenches behind the Canal, or rather behind a broad water-ditch which ran into the Canal.

The 2nd Manchesters, under Strickland,[1] late of the Norfolks, a first-rate battalion just arrived from India, had now been attached to the 14th Brigade—where their own 1st battalion were also—and had had very heavy fighting during the last few days just north of Festubert. The Devons were therefore sent to relieve them,—rather rough on them after barely forty-eight hours out of the trenches.

Oct. 29th.

We had an extraordinarily quiet night—a full eight hours' sleep without any disturbance,—and we were consequently feeling much fitter. But the ball began full early by a violent attack on the Devons at dawn, and another at 7 on the 2nd Manchesters, both hard pressed, but both repulsed—the Manchesters, who were short of ammunition, getting well in with the bayonet.

[1] Who had been with me as a Major in Belfast—a most capable officer, now (1917) commanding a Division.

I sent one company of the Norfolks to support the Devons, but I could barely afford even that. The enemy was entrenching within 200 to 400 yards of all my battalions, pushing out saps from their trenches along the ditches and folds of the ground, and connecting up their heads in a most ingenious and hidden manner. The French were not attacked, so they sent a couple of companies at my request to Les Plantins, behind the Norfolks. However, after another attack between 9 and 10 A.M. the Germans dried up for the present.

We knew that the Indian Divisions from Lahore and Meerut were shortly coming to strengthen this part of the line, and I was therefore not surprised to hear that Macbean, commanding one of their Brigades, wanted to see Martyn[1] and me about the relief of our respective Brigades. This was distinctly satisfactory from our point of view; but I was not entirely happy, for I was very doubtful how far these untried Indian troops would stand up to what was evidently going to be a very difficult situation if the Germans went on attacking as

---

[1] Temporarily commanding 13th Brigade.

N

they had been doing. Fresh troops, it is true. But they had had no experience of this sort of fighting, nor of trenches, nor of cold wet weather: and they were going to have all three.

The relief of the West Ridings by the Black Watch battalion of the Indian Division was carried out on the same evening. The relief of the Bedfords, Cheshires, and Dorsets was also arranged for, but the Norfolks could not be relieved till the morrow. The 2nd Manchesters were relieved, however, by the 2/8th Gurkhas, who looked very much out of place with their big hats and tiny, sturdy Mongolian physique.

Oct. 30th.

After a very quiet night — except for French guns which started shelling heavily about 4 A.M., and kept us awake till daylight—we had another unpleasant day.

There were repeated attacks on the Devons and Gurkhas all day, and at 3 P.M. Maynard reported that the Gurkhas had lost all their British officers and were being driven out of their trenches, and that support was badly wanted.

The first story about the Gurkhas was

that they had come to an end of their
ammunition and were fighting with the
bayonet, but were driven back by superior
numbers. But it turned out later that they
lost very heavily from shell fire, and, the
trenches being too deep for the little men,
they could produce no effect with their rifles,
and could see nothing. So, having lost all
their English officers, and being bewildered
by the heavy fire and totally new conditions,
and having no chance of getting in with
the bayonet, they cleared out one by one,
so as to get together into formation. The
Devons' last man was in the firing line by
this time, and so two Bedford companies and
the West Ridings, no longer under my command, were ordered to retake some Gurkha
trenches, into which the Germans had already
penetrated, alongside ours.

It was frightfully difficult to make out
what was happening, as not only were our
troops in process of being relieved by the
Indians, but there was very heavy fire as
well on all our supports and on the roads
leading up to the trenches, so that communication was all but impossible, most telephone
wires having been broken long ago and
found impossible to repair under such fire.

The 58th (Wilde's) Rifles had arrived, and were by way of relieving the Norfolks; but owing to this attack they were deflected in rear of the Devons. Then we were called on to send two companies to support the Devons. But, considering that they now had already two Bedford companies, four of West Ridings, and four of the 58th Rifles, to support them in enclosed country where they could hardly move, and that to weaken my already very thin line of Norfolks and Black Watch meant leaving me no supports at all, I respectfully protested, and gained my point.

Elaborate arrangements were made by the authorities for retaking the lost trenches by the Bedfords, &c., at nightfall; then the movement was deferred till 1.30 A.M., and then till dawn; but nothing happened at all during the night except occasional fire-bursts, which sounded like general attacks.

I might mention that during these "quiet" nights there were numerous fire-bursts at intervals, which used to bring me out of, or rather off, my bed three or four times a night, for the sentry on our cottage had strict orders to call me in case anything alarming occurred in our front. But they always slacked off after 5 or 10 minutes of my waiting in the cold, wet, muddy road, and I crept to bed again till the next one woke me.

It was a tiny cottage that we lived in during those days, belonging to a poor woman who, with her child, had been turned out by some one else and sent to another house half a mile off. She was perpetually coming back and weeping to be readmitted, but there really was not room, and we had to soothe her with promises, and eventually with cash in order to get rid of her. After all, she was living with her friends, though doubtless they were a bit crowded, and she returned to her cottage when we left it.

Everything in that country was mud, thick clay mud, black and greasy, and the country flat and hideous. And it rained perpetually and was getting beastly cold. Altogether it was a nightmare of a place, even without the fighting thrown in, and we prayed to be delivered from it, and go and fight somewhere else.

Our prayers were destined to be answered, for on this morning we were ordered, in spite of the desultory fighting going on, to hand over to Macbean's Brigade and go north. ' This only meant the Brigade Staff, two companies Bedfords, and about 300 Cheshires and 300 Dorsets who had been in reserve to the 14th Brigade; but they were not in a very happy condition, for they had hardly any officers left and had been extremely uncomfortable for the last week, being hauled out of their barns on most nights and made to sleep in the wet open as supports in case of attack.

Our orders were, together with the 15th R.F.A. Brigade, to move north and concentrate near Strazeele and Pradelles, where we were to go into rest for five or six days.

I knew those rests.

So after handing over to Macbean at 10.30 A.M., and talking to General Anderson (commanding the Indian Division) and the Maharajah of Bikanir,[1] we made devoutly thankful tracks in the direction of Locon and Merville.

We were but a small part of the 15th Brigade after all who left the environs of Festubert on that morning — only Headquarters, a very weak battalion of Cheshires

---

[1] I was struck with his wonderful command of English— not tho trace of any accent.

—not more than 300 all told—and two companies of Bedfords. The remains of the Dorsets had been ordered to join us about Strazeele, and the whole of the Norfolks and half the Bedfords were left in the trenches to give a bit of moral and physical support to the Indians. I did not at all like being parted from them, but there was no help for it. The West Ridings (Duke of Wellington's) were attached to me from the 13th Brigade, but that did not make up for the absence of one and a half of my own beloved battalions.

Nevertheless it was with a feeling of extreme thankfulness that we left the horrible mud-plain of Festubert and Givenchy, with its cold wet climate and its swampy surroundings and its dismal memories, for both Dorsets and Cheshires had suffered terribly in the fighting here. And the pleasantest feeling was to hear the noise of the bursting shells grow less and ever less as we worked north-westwards, and to realise that for the present, at all events, we need not worry about Jack Johnsons or Black Marias and all their numerous smaller brethren, nor to keep our attention on the tense strain for bad news from the firing trenches, but that we could, for

several days to come, sleep quietly, not
fully dressed and on our beds or straw
with one eye on the wake all night, but in
our blessed beds and in our still more beloved pyjamas.

We trotted on ahead over the cold, wet,
muddy, level roads of those parts, with a
welcome break for luncheon at a real live
estaminet, till we got to Merville, and then
we slowed down.

Merville is a nice prosperous little town,
with canals and parks and a distinctly good
modern statue of a French soldier in the
middle — by whom, and of whom, I have
forgotten.   It was, oddly enough, almost
like an extra - European bit of civilisation,
for the streets were swarming with Indians
and Africans of both armies—tall, solemn,
handsome Sikhs and Rajputs in khaki;
Spahis, Algerians, and Moors in every
variety of kit—red jackets, cummerbunds,
and baggy breeches, bright blue jackets,
white breeches, blue breeches, khaki breeches,
dark blue *vareuses*, white burnouses, Arab
corded turbans, baggy crimson trousers, &c.,
&c., even to Senegalese as black as night, and
Berbers from Mauritania and the Atlas. I
tried to talk to some of the latter, but it

was not a success, for they did not understand my Arabic, and I did not understand their Shlukh.

And so on *viâ* Strazeele—where Saunders and his Dorsets had already arrived—contentedly to Pradelle, in which neighbourhood we billeted, and were met by a staff officer, Cameron of the 5th Divisional Staff, who gave us the welcome news that we were to rest and recuperate for at least a week—really and truly this time.

We put up at a nice, bright, ugly little château belonging to an elderly lady who was most civil and told us stories of what the Germans had done when they passed through a week or two ago on their retreat eastwards. Amongst other abominations, they had, on arrival, demanded of the old curé the key of the church tower, on which they wished to put a Maxim. The old man, not having the key, had hobbled off to get it from the garde champêtre, who happened to be in possession of it for the time being. He could not, however, find him, and the officer in command, being in a diabolical temper, put the poor old priest up against a wall and shot him dead on the spot. This was recounted by the curé's sister, and

there was not a shadow of doubt on the
matter, for it was confirmed by all.

Oct. 31st.

Next day was a clear bright Sunday, and
before we had come down to breakfast,
looking forward to a nice lazy day, we
were ordered to send the Dorsets away
in motor - buses to Wulverghem (opposite
Messines), where heavy fighting was going
on. So much for our promised week's rest!
And before 11 o'clock we had received another urgent telegram telling us to fall in
at once and march eastwards through
Bailleul.

I was deputed to command the whole of
the remaining troops of the Division on
this march, and by a complicated series of
moves from their billets we got them strung
out on the road, and pushed on by 12.30.
The troops were mostly artillery, engineers,
and train, and the only other infantry that
joined me were the West Kent, now under
their own C.O., Martyn.

Other troops were also on the move
through Bailleul, and we had a weary time
of it getting through. It was dark before
we had filed through the big market-square

with its old brick church tower and Town
Hall; and even then, though billets had
been arranged for in the country beyond
for the rest of the troops, we had the
devil's own job before our own headquarters
could find a resting-place. We wanted to
put up at Dranoutre village, but the village
was full of the 3rd Cavalry Brigade, and
we should have been in front of our own
lot; so after a depressing wait in a tiny
pothouse near Dranoutre, whilst St André
and Weatherby and Moulton-Barrett scoured
the country, we eventually settled down in
a little farmhouse at Hille, a few hundred
yards inside the Belgian border. Not so
bad, but tiny, and crowded with not only
the proprietor and his numerous family, but
with a number of refugees from further east.
My own bedroom was about 6 feet square
and full of stinking old clothes, but I was
lucky to get one at all.

It seemed curious being amongst inhabitants many of whom understood no French,
but only talked Wallon or Flemish. I found
my reminiscences of the South African Taal
came in quite usefully; but the best com-
municators were the Lowland Scots, who,
thanks to their own strange dialect, managed

to make themselves quite decently understood by the natives.

Here we stayed for a few days—to be
accurate, until the morning of the 5th
November. My own "outfit" consisted of
the West Kent, Cheshires, and two companies Bedfords, and the West Ridings
were subsequently added. At one period I
was given the K.O.S.B.'s as well, who were
in Neuve Eglise; but they were taken away
from me on the same day, and so were the
West Kent. There was, in fact, a glorious
jumble, battalions and batteries being added
and taken away as the circumstances demanded. Even the two companies Bedfords
were spirited away for forty - eight hours,
leaving me with the decimated Cheshires
as the only representatives of the 15th
Brigade, but with two battalions of the
13th and one of the 14th superadded, as
well as an R.E. company (17th). Meanwhile
the 5th Divisional Staff was stranded 'and
almost troopless, for all the other battalions
of the Division were scattered among other
divisions — some even under the command
of the Cavalry Division; and guns were
pushed up, almost piecemeal, as they were
wanted, to help in the attempt to retake

Messines, out of which our cavalry had been driven some days before. French troops were also there, in lumps. One morning the country would be brilliant with the white horses, sky-blue tunics and red trousers, of the Chasseurs d'Afrique, and the roads impassable with French infantry and transport moving towards Ypres; and by the next evening nothing but khaki-clad British were seen, besides patches of Belgian infantry, largely stragglers and mostly unarmed.

Meanwhile rumours of desperate fighting up north came through — the critical time when the 7th Division stuck heroically to their crippled trenches and withstood the ponderous attacks of the German masses; but it was difficult to make out what was occurring, for one only gathered bits of news here and there and could not piece them together as a whole, for the links were missing.

On the 4th November we received orders that Sir Horace would inspect us on the following morning, and we made preparations to turn out as clean as we could in the ever-prevailing mud. But in the evening more important work was at hand, for we were notified to be ready to march on the following morning to Ypres. So the inspection fell through.

The idea was that we—that is, two companies Bedfords (450 men), Cheshires (550), and West Ridings (700)—were to combine as the 15th Brigade with M'Cracken's 7th Brigade (Wiltshires, Gordons, Irish Rifles, and another battalion), and go to relieve the 7th Division, which had, we heard, been getting some terrific knocks. With us were to go the two R.E. companies, the 17th and 59th, belonging to the 5th Division.

Nov. 5th.

We marched at 7.20 A.M. *vid* Locres and Dickebusch, on the main Bailleul - Ypres road, passing through many French troops on the way. Not far on the other side of Dickebusch we heard that the road was being shelled by the enemy; so M'Cracken ordered the whole force to park in the fields some distance down a road to the west, whilst he went on to Ypres for instructions.

We had our midday meal whilst we waited there, but it was not pleasant for the men, for the fields were dripping wet and very muddy; they had, therefore, to sit on their kits, whilst the transport had to remain on the road, the fields being so deep.

M'Cracken came back at 3.30 P.M. with instructions, and we moved on, myself being in charge of the movement. We managed to get to Ypres all right along the main road, as the shells were rather diminishing and not reaching so far, and we pushed through the town, entering it by a bridge over the nearly dry canal. Why the Germans had not shot this bridge to pieces before I cannot imagine, as it was well within their range. There were numerous big shell-holes in the open space near the railway station; one or two houses were smouldering; there were heaps of bricks and stones from damaged houses in the streets, and the extreme roof corner of the Cloth Hall had been knocked off, but other-wise the town was fairly normal - looking, except, of course, that hardly any civilians were visible.

At the other end of the town I came across General Haig, and rode ahead with him down the Menin road as far as the village of Hooge, where the Headquarters of the 1st Division were, under General Landon. (He had succeeded General Lomax,

who had been badly wounded by a shell
exploding at his headquarters, and subsequently died, 15th April.) Here we had a
cup of tea in a dirty little estaminet crowded
with Staff officers whilst awaiting the arrival
of the Brigade.

No part of this Menin road was, in fact,
"healthy," and at night it was generally
subject to a searching fire by German shells.
The wonder, indeed, was that more casualties did not occur here, for after dark the
road was packed with transport and ration
and ambulance parties moving slowly and
silently back and forth. But the hostile
shelling was not accurate, and for one
"crumper" that burst in or over the road
twenty exploded in the fields alongside.

Only a day or two before, a couple of
heavy shells had burst just outside General
Haig's Headquarters at the entrance to
Ypres. Luckily the General himself had
just left, but poor "Conky" Marker of the
Coldstream had been fatally wounded, and
several other officers, signallers, and clerks
had been killed.

My Brigade arrived in the dark by the time
that I had received further instructions in
detail, and was parked off the road (south

side) half a mile further on, whilst Weatherby went on to make arrangements for their taking up the line, taking representatives of the battalions with him. I met General Capper (commanding 7th Division) at his dug-out in the wood close by, and he told me that his Division had been reduced to barely 3000 men and a very few officers, after an appalling amount of severe fighting.

Weatherby came back after a time, and the battalions and ourselves moved off along the road and branched off into the grounds of Herenthage Château—deep mud, broken trees, and hardly rideable. Here we bade adieu to our horses, who were, with the transport, to stay in the same place where we had had our dinners, right the other side of Ypres and out of shell-range, whilst we kept a few ammunition-carts and horses hidden near Hooge village. All the rest of our supplies and stuff had to be brought up every night under cover of darkness to near Herenthage, and there be unloaded and carried by hand into the trenches.

In the château itself who should we come across but Drysdale,[1] Brigade-Major now

[1] My late Brigade-Major at Belfast, now, alas ! killed (on the Somme, 1916).

O

of the 22nd Brigade, the one which, by the law of chances, we were now relieving; and, still more oddly, the other battalion (2nd) of the Bedfords was in his Brigade. It was a cheerless place, this château—every single pane of glass in it shivered, and lying, crunched at our every step, on the floor.

We pushed on over the grass of the park, through the scattered trees, and into the wood, and so into the trenches. Even then, as far as one could judge in the darkness, the ground was a regular rabbit-warren. By the time we had finished with the district the ground was even more so; there seemed to be more trenches and fallen trees and wire entanglements than there was level ground to walk on.

Our own Headquarters were in a poky little dug-out[1] in a wood, not 200 yards from our firing trenches. There was just room for two—Weatherby and St André (Moulton-Barrett having gone to settle about transport and supplies, Cadell being away sick, and Beilby being left with the transport the other side of Ypres)—to lie down in it, and there was a little tunnel out of it,

[1] Really only a half roofed-in little trench, marked H on the map.

6 feet long and 2 broad and 2 high, into
which I crept and where I slept; but I
was not very happy in it, as the roof-logs
had sagged with the weight of the earth

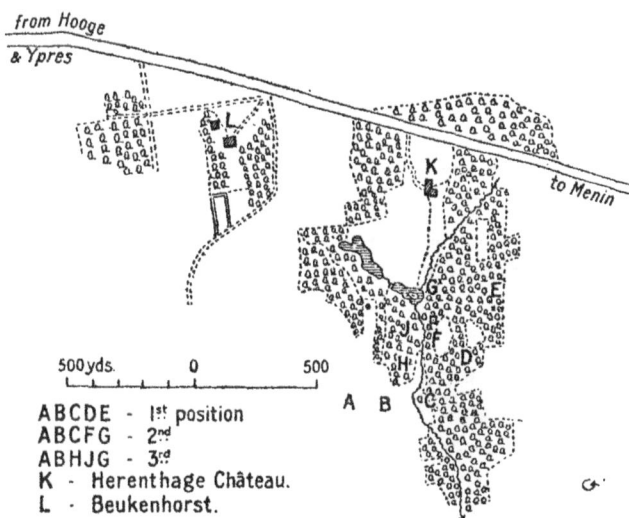

ABCDE - 1st position
ABCFG - 2nd
ABHJG - 3rd
K - Herenthage Château.
L - Beukenhorst.

on them, and threatened every moment to
fall in whilst I was inside.

The Bedfords were put into the trenches
on the eastern edge of the wood, the
Cheshires continued the line to the south
and for a couple of hundred yards outside
the wood, and the West Ridings were in

reserve at the back of the wood, in rear of our dug-out.

I did not like our place at all, for it seemed to me that, being so close to the firing line, I should not be able to get out or control the little force if there were heavy operations on; and this was exactly what did happen.

We had been told that the 6th Cavalry Brigade was in trenches on our left, and the 7th Infantry Brigade in ditto on our right, and that was about all we knew of the situation.

Nov. 6th.

Next morning there was a thick mist till 10 A.M., and I took advantage of it to visit the trenches in detail. The left of the Cheshires was within 40 yards of the enemy, who were hidden in the wood in front of them, so, there being no communication trenches, we had to be fairly careful hereabouts. But it was desperately difficult to make one's way about, what with the fallen trees and telephone wires, and little patches of open ground on the slopes, and long, wet, yellow grass and tangled heather in parts, not to mention

the criss - cross of trenches, occupied and
unoccupied, in all directions. Difficult
enough to find one's way in daylight, it
was infinitely worse in pitch darkness. No
wonder that our reliefs had not been accom-
plished till nearly 3 o'clock that morning!

We were shelled pretty heavily all the
morning, and two of the shells burst so
close that they covered us with dirt. Two
officers—Langdale and O'Kelly, of the West
Ridings — had their legs broken by their
dug - out being blown in upon them, and
three Cheshires were buried by an exploding shell and dug out dead. Another dozen
were killed or wounded in their trenches,
which were nothing like deep enough,
and could not be further deepened because
of the water which lay there only just
below the ground. About twenty Cheshires
were moved back to escape the shell fire, and
taken to a rather less - exposed place. At
4.30 the Bedfords reported a heavy attack
on their front; but it was confined to rifle
fire, and nothing serious happened there.

The remainder of the Bedfords, under
Griffith, consisting of two strong companies,
turned up at 6 P.M., and the West Ridings
were taken away from me, so that my

command was now reduced to two battalions, one rather strong (1100—just reinforced by a big fresh draft), and the other,
Cheshires, only about half that number.

On further consideration of the situation,
I settled to make Brigade Headquarters
at the Beukenhorst Château,[1] half a mile
farther back, and started the R.E. and a
strange fatigue party to dig a funk-hole
for us in front of it in case it were badly
shelled; but I remember as a particular
grievance that when the foreign fatigue
party heard they were to go somewhere
else, they went off, leaving their work half
undone, and with our Brigade tools, though
I had given them distinct orders to do
neither of these things. But they were
now out of my jurisdiction, so nothing
could be done except to send them a
message to return our tools—which they
never did.

Moulton-Barrett turned up in the afternoon with a basket of cold food for us,
and took St André away; it was not the
least necessary for him to stay, as the dug-
out was really only big enough for two, so
Weatherby and I settled down for the night.

---

[1] "Stirling Castle" on our present maps.

We had wanted to move into the château at 7 P.M., but we could not. For it was not advisable as long as an attack was imminent; also, M. B. had not got our message of that morning saying we wanted him to clean up the château for us; and thirdly, the Bedford relief was taking place. So we settled to move next day instead.

But it was not very attractive living in the tiny dug-out. We had no servants, we had to prepare our own food and wash up afterwards; it was frightfully cramped, and we were always getting half-empty sardine-tins oozing over official documents, and knives and forks lost in the mud and straw at the bottom, and bread-crumbs and fragments of bully beef and jam mixed up with our orders and papers; and it was not at all healthy going for a stroll as long as the sun was up because of the bullets and shells fizzing about. Altogether, although it was no worse, except as regards size, than other dug-outs, it was not luxurious; and as for washing, a little water in the bottom of a biscuit-tin was about all we could manage, whilst a shave was a matter of pain and difficulty.

Nov. 7th.

We had now come under the 3rd Division (under General Wing temporarily — a very good and charming fellow, a gunner, who had taken over General Hubert Hamilton's command, the latter having been killed, I forgot to mention, some time previously), whilst the 9th Brigade had relieved the 6th Cavalry on the previous day. The Division, therefore, now consisted of the 7th, 15th, and 9th Brigades (the latter comprising the Northumberland Fusiliers, Royal Fusiliers, Lincolns, and Scots Fusiliers) —in that order from right to left. It looked, therefore, as if we ought to be soon relieved by the 8th Brigade and return to our own Division. Vain hope! We were not destined to be relieved for another fortnight.

There was a good deal of shelling of the 9th Brigade during the morning, but we personally had not many shells into us, and were fairly quiet till past 2 o'clock.

Suddenly, about 3, a hellish hostile fire broke out in the wood—not in our front, but close on our left. A hail of bullets whizzed over our heads, responded to by our fire trenches; and then, to our horror, we saw our Bedford supports, to our left

front, retiring slowly, but in some confusion, on top of us—many of the men only
half-dressed, and buckling on their kits as
they moved. We jumped out of our dug-
out, and with the assistance of their officers
stopped and rallied them. They were certainly not running, and were in no sort of
panic; but they all said that the word had
been passed from the right front that the
Bedfords were to retire, so they had done
so—half of them being asleep or feeding at
the time the fire began.

We made them advance again, which they
were more than willing to do, and then
there was a cheer from the Bedfords in
front. Upon which the supports pricked
up their ears, rallied to the sound, and
charged forward like hounds rallying to
the horn.

Violent firing and confused fighting and
yelling in the wood for a space, and some
wounded began to come back. Then some
Germans, both wounded and prisoners, in
small batches, and at last the news that
the Bedfords had completely repulsed the
attack and taken about 25 prisoners, driving
the enemy back with the bayonet at the run.

Who it was that started the order to

retire we could never find out. It certainly
was not Milling, who was commanding
in the front trench, nor was it any officer.
Quite conceivably it may have been started
by the enemy themselves.

What happened, as far as I could make
out, was that the right centre of the Northumberland Fusiliers on our left had been
pressed back and the Germans had poured
through the opening. The right flank of
the Northumberlands had sat tight, so the
Bedfords in our front line had known
nothing of the German success till they
were fired at by the enemy in the wood
on their left rear. I do not fancy, however,
from what the prisoners told me, that the
attack was a very strong one—not more,
I expect, than three or four companies.

These belonged to the Frankfurt-am-Main
Corps (VII.). I examined one prisoner, a
regular "Schwabe" from Heilbronn, a jolly
man with a red beard, who told me that
his company was commanded by a cavalry
captain, who considered it beneath his
dignity to charge with infantry, and remained snugly ensconced behind a wall
whilst he shouted encouragement to his
men.

The Bedfords retook three of the North-umberlands' trenches with them, but failed to retake one of their own—together with two machine-guns in it—that they had lost, although they tried hard, A Company (Milling's) making three bayonet charges. They behaved devilish well, in spite of heavy losses both in officers and men. Macready, their Adjutant, was shot through the liver (but recovered eventually); Allason (Major) was hit twice — once through the shoulder, and again, on returning after getting his wound dressed, through the thigh; Davenport was shot through the left elbow (we looked after him in our dug-out); and two subalterns were killed, besides twenty-four men killed and fifty-three wounded. Of the Cheshires, Pollok, Hodson, and Anderson (the latter a fine runner and very plucky chap) were killed, besides five men killed, nineteen wounded, and eight missing. Altogether the losses were rather heavy. The men were partic-ularly good to the wounded Germans; I remember especially one man, a black-bearded evil-looking scoundrel, who had been shot through the lungs, and rolled about in the mud at my feet, and him they looked after carefully. The last glimpse I caught of him was being helped to a stretcher by two of our own men, also wounded.

There was again no chance of our getting to the château to-night, so another basket of food arrived, and we fed with what comfort we could.

We worked all night at strengthening our lines, but the Germans had got up so close to our weakest salient that I was a bit anxious on the subject of a renewed attack by night.

Nov. 8th.

A small reinforcement arrived at 7 A.M., in the shape of the Divisional Mounted Troops of the 3rd and 5th Divisions—about 250 men altogether, consisting of 70 of the 15th Hussars and 60 cyclists from the 3rd, and 50 of the 19th Hussars and 70 cyclists from the 5th Divisions, under Courage and Parsons respectively.

These were distributed in rear of our dug-out.

We had a fairly quiet day as far as we ourselves were concerned, but both Brigades on our flanks were heavily shelled. The

French on our right were attacking in force, but although they were being supported by their 16th Corps, I do not think there was much result about Klein Zillebeke.

At last, at 5.30 P.M., we started for our château, and hardly had we gone 150 yards when a terrific fire broke out. We got behind a little ruined hut to escape the bullets, and I made ready to return in case it was a serious attack. But it died down in ten minutes, and we pursued our way in more or less peace, for it was only a case of firing at reliefs, and I think the Germans were rather jumpy.

The Château of Beukenhorst was a square white block of a place, and merits perhaps some description, as we were there for a most uncomfortable fortnight—uncomfortable as far as events and fighting went, though not so as regards living.

It belonged to some people whose name I have forgotten—Baron something (Belgian) and his German wife, and it was due to this lady's nationality—so the story went—that the place had suffered so little. Personally I think that it was due to the house only being indicated on the map, whilst the stables, 200 yards off, which were perpetually being shelled, were marked in heavy black, and were a cockshy for the German guns, which were evidently laid by map and not by sight; yet the house was on a fair elevation, and must have been visible from certain points on the German side. By the same token, General Capper had had his Headquarters there for a few days, but had cleared out, I believe, because of shells. Half a dozen shrapnel had certainly hit it, but they had only chipped off some bits of stone and broken all the windows at the eastern end.

We lived in a room half below ground at the western end, which must evidently have been the housekeeper's room or servants' hall, next to the kitchen. About half the Signal Section lived in some sort of cellars close by, the other half being away with the transport. Two of these cellars were also used as a dressing station for the 7th Brigade, and wounded used to be brought in here frequently and tended by a sanitary Highlander, a corporal whose exact functions I could never discover, but who worked like a Trojan. The wounded were visited by a medical officer in the evening, and removed on stretchers every night to the ambulances who came to fetch them. Our own wounded did not come here, but were looked after just behind the trenches near the Herenthage Château, and taken away from there at night by our own 15th Field Ambulance, who worked all night in circumstances of much danger, but were luckily hardly ever hit.

The owners had evidently had plenty of notice before clearing out, for they had removed all the smaller articles and most of the furniture, and had rolled up the carpets and curtains and blinds, leaving only big cupboards and bare bedsteads and larger bits of furniture. These were, oddly enough, in very good taste — Louis XV. style — and only sand - papered and not polished or painted. There was a good bathroom too, and a lavatory with big basins, but much of it had been smashed by shrapnel, as it was at the east end. Our bedrooms were on the first floor, and most of them had good beds and washhand-stands, but no linen or blankets. I need hardly say that we carefully selected those at the western end of the house, whither few bullets had penetrated. But the windows there were mostly untouched, and consisted

of good plate glass. Altogether the whole
place gave one the idea of comfort, money,
and good taste, and was an eminently
satisfactory abode—bar the shells.

I know that, as far as looking after the
Brigade was concerned, we got through
three times as much satisfactory work in
the morning after we arrived as we did
during all the three days we were in the
little dug-out. For we could now communicate not only by wire but by messenger
and by personal contact with the authorities and commanders in our rear and on
our flanks, and could discuss matters *re*
artillery and defences and plans in a way
which had been quite impossible in our
advanced position.

General Wing[1] used to come and see us
most evenings, and I used to communicate
personally with Shaw (9th Brigade), and
Fanshawe (Artillery), and M'Cracken (7th
Brigade), about combined movements, &c.
Every morning before daylight, and at a
good many other times besides, I, or
Weatherby, or Moulton-Barrett, used to go
down to the trenches and confabulate with

[1] To everybody's great regret, he was killed in October
1915.

Griffith—always cool and resourceful, who was in immediate command — or Frost and Burfeild, who were running the Cheshires excellently between them. It was not always a very easy business getting down to the trenches, for there were nearly always shells bursting in the woods and on the open field which lay between us and the trench wood; and we had generally to hurry in order to leave the château precincts unperceived by the beastly Taubes who hovered overhead, always on the lookout for headquarters to shell; so we cut down orderlies and staff to a minimum, and absolutely forbade any hanging about outside.

It is no use going into or describing our proceedings day by day: "Plus ça changeait, plus c'était la même chose." I have the detail of it day by day in my diary, but it was always, in the main, the same thing—minds and bodies at high tension throughout the day and most of the night; perpetual artillery fire—if not by the enemy then by ourselves; shells bursting round the château and hardly ever into it, mostly shrapnel near the house and Black Marias a bit further off — chiefly into a walled garden 200 yards off which, for some unknown reason, the Germans were convinced held some of our guns, though, as a matter of fact, our batteries were in our right rear, in well-covered positions just inside (or even outside, in some cases) the woods. But we got shells on the other side of the house as well, over the bare half-grown lawn and flower-beds between the château and the Hooge-Menin road.

It was rarely "healthy" to take a stroll in the grounds, however much we might be in want of fresh air.   Even on days which were exceptionally quiet—and there were not many of them,—when one would move out to look at the grounds with a view to future defences in case we were driven back, or with a desire to ease a torpid liver, suddenly there would be a loudening swish in the air and a crash which would send one of the tall pine-trees into smithereens, with a shower of broken branches in all directions, followed by another, or half a dozen more; and we would retire gracefully — sometimes even rapidly—behind the shelter of our house.

There were some late roses in the garden, or rather in the scattered flower-beds near the house, which lasted out even when the

snow was on them; but about the only live
beings who took any interest in them were
three or four goats, who haunted the precincts of the château, and were everlastingly
trying to get inside. Indeed, when Moulton-
Barrett first came to take possession, there
were two goats in the best bedrooms up-
stairs, who peered out of the windows at
the undesired visitors, and had to be evicted
after a display of considerable force.

Also pigs; for half a dozen great raw-
boned pink and dirty swine rootled about
in the woods near by for sustenance. They
were, however, shy, and did not seek the
shelter of the château. Stray cattle there
were too; but neither these nor the pigs
paid any attention to the shells which fell
near them with impartial regularity, but
did them, as far as I could see, no damage
whatever.

There was a stable a couple of hundred
yards in rear of the house, and here at first
we put what horses there were in the
neighbourhood. Having Squeaky and Silver
there one night—I forget why, but I know
they were there—I put them into a couple
of loose-boxes. Silver went in all right,
but Squeaky, generally a most sensible

mare, shivered and sweated with terror, had almost to be forced in, and refused to feed when there. So I let her out again, and picketed her outside. Two nights after, a doctor's horse which was in there was all but killed, for a shrapnel burst through the window and drove fourteen bullets into his head and neck. They wanted leave to kill the poor beast, but I refused permission, as he was not hit in any vital spot, and he recovered, more or less, in a few days.

As mentioned above, this stable was marked in black on the map, whilst the château—a far bigger building, of course— was hardly indicated. I take it that this accounted for our comparative immunity, for the stable was shelled (and hit) with great regularity, whilst the château was hardly ever touched. We had, however, a couple of small H.E. shell through the eastern end whilst we were in the western; one of these bored clean through the wall of a room where there was a big cupboard against it on the far side and exploded forthwith. But the cupboard was not even scratched; it was blown into the middle of the room and a table or two upset, but, strange to relate, nothing serious in the way of damage

was done.[1] On another occasion, however,
a few shrapnel exploded just outside the
kitchen window. At the sound of the first
we all bolted to the other side of the house,
and called to the servants to do the same.
They came out; but Brown, our excellent
cook, who had come out in his shirt-sleeves,
must needs go back, without orders, to fetch
his coat: for which he promptly received
a jagged piece of shell in his left arm, which
put a stop, alas, to his cooking for good and
all, as far as we were concerned, for he was
sent away, and, although he recovered, never
came back to us.

During the chief hours of the day, when
not (or whilst) being shelled, we were pretty
busy with telegrams and reports and queries
and excursions and alarums. We were comfortable enough in the housekeeper's room,
and got our meals "reg'lar," and we even
had two or three arm-chairs, and newspapers
and mails fairly well, and news from outside,
which used to arrive with our rations at 9
P.M. or thereabouts. But a minor trial was
the fact that two out of our five panes of
glass had been blown in by shell, and let in
an icy draught on most days. So we got

[1] This is a fact, though I cannot explain it.

some partially-oiled paper, and made some paste, and stuck up the panes.

The first shell explosion made the paper sag, the second made it shiver, and the third blew it out. The paste would not stick—it was the wrong sort of flour or something.

Then we used jam—that glutinous saccharine mess known as " best plum jam"— and blue sugar paper, and it stuck quite fairly well. But it wouldn't dry; and tears of jam used to trickle down the paper panes and mingle with the tin-tacks and the bread-crumbs on the sill.

The room was even then fairly dark, but the shell-bursts again shivered the jam paper and burst it, and we had to take to cardboard and drawing-boards. This made it still darker, and was not even then successful, for the explosions still shook the boards down and eventually broke another pane: it was most trying. On the last day but one four panes had been broken, and on the last day, as will be recounted, all were broken and the whole window blown in. Then we left.

But what was of much vaster interest, of course, than these trifles, was the desperate fighting which was being waged along our front, not 1000 yards from the château. Our two battalions, being entrenched in the wood, did not receive such a severe hammering as the brigades on either side—the 7th and 9th respectively on our right and left,—who were more in the open. And the shelling and attacks on them were incessant, as well as on troops still further off on the other side of them.

The 11th November was a typically unpleasant day. It started with a touch of comedy, Weatherby arriving stark naked in my room at 6.30 A.M., just when I was shaving, saying, "I say, sir, may I finish my dressing in here? They're shelling the bathroom!" He had a towel and a few clothes on his arm, *et præterea nihil*. (He, M.-B., and St André, though sleeping in different rooms, used to dress in the bathroom, where there were excellent taps and basins, though no water was running.)

The shelling continued till 10. It was on this morning that Brown was damaged and lots of windows blown in.

About that time I saw, to my consternation, a number of British soldiers retiring towards the walled garden. I sent out at once to stop them and turn them back, thinking

they were Cheshires or Bedfords. To my
relief they were neither, but belonged to
a brigade on our right. They had been
heavily shelled, and, though in no sort of
panic, were falling back deliberately, though
without orders. There were no officers with
them—all killed or wounded, I believe. My
efforts were successful, though I grieve to
say that a nice boy, Kershaw of the
Signallers, who volunteered to carry a
message to them, was hit by shrapnel in the
thigh and brought in by our clerk, Sergeant
Hutchison, and another, bleeding profusely.
Burnett, commanding the Cyclist Corps, had
been knocked down by a falling tree and
his back damaged—also internal damage, I
believe (for he was not really fit a year
afterwards); he also was brought in, as
well as Cooper of the Royal Fusiliers. A
number of Zouaves and some more troops
also trickled slowly back from the left with
stories of appalling losses (mostly untrue)
and disaster to the trenches (ditto). They
were also stopped—the Zouaves by St André
—and sent back. Certainly the French-
men's nerve was not damaged, for I remember that several had playing-cards in
their hands, and when they got to what

they considered a fairly quiet spot they
stopped, sat down, and went on with their
game. Norman M'Mahon, commanding
Royal Fusiliers, had, however, been killed,
just as he had been appointed Brigadier to
another Brigade, besides a lot more good
men of the 9th Brigade. Shaw, commanding the Brigade, had also been wounded,
and Douglas Smith succeeded him. Both
the 1st and 9th Brigades had lost several
trenches, and intended to try and retake
them at night, but both had been pushed
back some distance.

A company of Wiltshires was sent to
reinforce us in case we were seriously
attacked. But they were not used by us
for fighting—only for digging extra trenches
near the château in case the front battalions
had to fall back. But the front battalions
had no intention of falling back, and the
Cheshires got in a very heavy fire on the
flank of some Germans who were attacking the 7th Brigade, and, together with the
Gordons on our right, killed a great number.
The Cheshires reported afterwards that the
Germans walked slowly forward to the
attack without enthusiasm and in a sort
of dazed way, with their rifles under their

arms, as if they were drugged. I wonder whether they were: we several times received reports to the same effect.

A particularly cheery item of intelligence, on good authority, was that fifteen German Guards battalions were being specially brought up in order to break through our line here at all costs. I thought at the time that this was false news, and that nothing like so many would be available, but it was not far out. As part confirmation, some papers taken off a dead German officer were brought in; they belonged to A. von Obernitz, 2nd Garde Grenadier Regiment, 2nd Division Guard Corps, but there was nothing of interest in them.

About that date Weatherby, who had been seedy for several days, became seriously ill with a sort of light typhoid fever, and had to be evacuated. Moulton-Barrett therefore added the duties of Brigade-Major to his already heavy ones as Staff Captain, and did excellently well in the double capacity.

To finish up with, the weather, which had been calm and fine up to date, broke that evening, and there were violent rain-storms from the south-west all night.

We went to bed in no very happy state of

mind, expecting a serious night attack by overwhelming forces. But no attack came, for probably the enemy was as exhausted as ourselves. All the same we had to fall back by order, on the following night, for many trenches on our right and left had been driven in, and we did not want to be cut off.

So we fell back about 200 yards through the wood, and straightened up our line—in a much worse defensive position as regards our own bit, but it could not be helped. My suggestions as to the line were overruled, and we took up our second line of trenches and constructed a little réduit in the wood, ringed around with barbed wire and holding about twenty-five men, who would—we were sanguine enough to expect — hold off any serious rush that came.

I forgot to mention that Singer, commanding the 17th Fd. Co. R.E., had arrived, and did an extraordinary amount of good work with his company in circumstances of the greatest difficulty and danger. He told me that the first night he went out, in order to put up some wire entanglement in a dangerous place, it was as black as pitch. He made his sections hold on to each other's coats, but within ten minutes they had not only lost each other in the dense black woods—chiefly through tumbling into trenches and falling over telephone wires,—but Singer had lost the whole company, and after wandering helplessly in what he thought the right direction for some time, he discovered that he had lost himself as well. He said he felt inclined to sit down and have a good cry, so utterly miserable did he feel!

In falling back to the second line we had a fairly easy job, but for the 9th Brigade it was a regular Chinese puzzle, for by this time some of their trenches were in German hands at one end and English at the other, whilst Northumberland Fusiliers, Lincolns, Sussex, West Ridings, Cavalry, and even part of the 2nd Grenadiers,[1] who had turned up from goodness knows where, were inextricably tangled up; not to mention that a party of Northumberlands, numbering about 120, under one gallant subaltern called Brown, had been holding out for three days in front of our line, with no food or drink, and Germans in trenches only 30 yards off them. I believe this lot eventually got away in safety, but the

[1] My old battalion.

retirement of all was about as difficult as
it could be. This was on the 13th.

On the 14th the Bedfords were heavily
attacked, and the Germans pushed a machine-
gun right forward through the wood and
enfiladed the Cheshire left. These stood it
for some time and then retired further down
their trench, being unable to let the Bedfords
know. Consequently this beastly gun got in
a heavy fire on the Bedfords right as well
and forced them to retire. The réduit was
no good — the wood was too thick — and
some of the garrison were captured. So
the Bedfords had to fall back, fighting, on
to their third line 50 yards back, where
they held the enemy.

Edwards, who commanded the advanced
Bedford company, came up to the château
to report, and gave a most cheery and
amusing account of the whole thing, but
the result was not at all amusing, as we
had lost ground and a lot of men.

Meanwhile the big attack by the German
Guards was being made on the brigades on
our flanks, but, as all the world knows, it
was completely repulsed, though the 15th
Brigade was not very heavily engaged as a
whole. The fighting was terribly confused

in the woods, and nothing but the individual grit of our men held the line, for it was practically impossible to give directions or exercise control in this horrible terrain.

During this period we got much "mixed" as regards our machine-guns. We took over some from the 7th Division and lost some of those. Then we borrowed some more from other units in rear and recovered some of the lost ones. Sergeant Mart of the Bedfords did a splendid thing, and recovered two of the lost Bedford guns practically by himself, stalking the Germans with only one other man and rushing their trench, killing the few men in it. I wanted to recommend him for the V.C., but had such difficulty in getting sufficient evidence about it that an official recommendation would not have held water. Meanwhile poor Mart was shot through the neck. I got him a D.C.M., but do not know whether he lived to receive it.

Then three out of our five guns got damaged by shells and bullets and mud and stopped work. So we borrowed some more, and had some difficulty in working them, as they were a new pattern. By the time we understood them two other guns were *hors de combat,*—it was a real nightmare, and it needed strenuous efforts to keep even one or two guns[1] going; yet they were of enormous importance, and accounted for a lot of the enemy, especially on the right flank of the Cheshires.

Meanwhile the weather had turned beastly cold—snowstorms and sleet during the day and a hard frost at night. The men suffered terribly in the trenches — especially the Cheshires, whose trenches were very wet. Although we kept the wet ones occupied as lightly as possible, we could not abandon them altogether and dig others further forward or back, as there was water everywhere only a foot below the ground. Breastworks were attempted, but they were very visible and attracted large numbers of shells: altogether the Cheshires had a very poor time, I fear. The Bedfords were rather better off, their trenches in the wood being on rather higher and sandy ground, but they were not dry by any means.

It was very awkward getting to the trenches, even in broad daylight, by this time,

---

[1] It does indeed seem extraordinary now that in those strenuous days of 1914 we only had about three machine-guns to two battalions. Nowadays we should have at least twenty !

for such numbers of trees had been blown
down by the shells, there were so many shell-
holes and so much wire about, and the mud
and pools of water so universal, that it was
really quite a physical effort to get through
at all.

About this time—the 17th—the Germans
in our immediate front appeared to have
retired a bit, but they certainly had not
gone far, for our scouts on pushing on for
50 yards or so were greeted with a heavy
fire, so we were unable to get on as much
as we wanted. But though the rifle-bullets
were rarer for a day or two, shells certainly
were not, and continued with the utmost
regularity.

On the evening of the 17th, by the way,
the enemy, annoyed perhaps at our scouts
pushing on, made what was probably meant
to be a counter-attack. It was not made
in much strength, and we repelled it with
ease. But it appeared to us at the château
to be more serious than it was, for a
messenger from the trenches arrived with
the information that the Bedfords were
being very severely pressed, and the
Cheshires had had very heavy losses, and
could not hold their trenches for more than

ten minutes unless they were supported at once. I had no supports to send them. A message to Griffith by telephone for confirmation of this alarm produced no result, for the wires were, of course, broken at that critical moment. So I wired to General Wing asking him to send me some supports if he could, and got 200 Royal Fusiliers shortly afterwards. But I did not use them, for the news of the messenger—who protested that he had been sent with a verbal message (not likely) by an officer whose name he did not know—turned out to be grossly exaggerated, and by the time the Fusiliers arrived the fighting was over. I never could trace whether any officer was responsible for the original message: I believe not. Anyhow, there was trouble for the messenger.

On the 18th and 19th we had comparatively quiet days—except for nervousness about our left flank, where certain troops who had joined the 9th Brigade were very heavily shelled and lost one or two of their trenches. They managed, indeed, to get most of the lost ground back, but I was not entirely happy about it, for the ground between us and them was extremely difficult and could not be properly covered by either

Q

of us. There was a pond hereabouts, with a little island on it with a summer-house; and we found, on extending our left to take it over, that there must have been a German sniper there for several nights, for many empty Mauser cartridge - cases were found in the summer-house, and a very dicky punt was discovered in the rushes. This latter we sank, and were no more troubled; but it shows the cool pluck of the enemy's snipers in getting right into our lines by themselves (and also — I regret to add— certain other things as well).

Rumours now came of an approaching relief, and certainly troops had rarely been more in want of it, for our two battalions had been in the trenches for fourteen days, with pretty stiff fighting — and nervous, jumpy fighting in the dark at that—all the time, and no chance of being comfortable or quiet during the whole of this period. Each battalion had had to find its own supports or reserves; but even the latter had to be pretty close up to the firing line, for in such cramped country one could not afford the risk of a sudden rush which might have succeeded before the reserves could get up. Our line, it is true, was not a particularly long one; but it was awkward, and the troops were much cramped and confined by nearly all being obliged to take cover in the wood, which gradually grew too small to hold them.

Nov. 19th.

On the 19th General Wing arrived and told us that, after settling to relieve us to-day, the French had been unable to find the men and could not do it. This was a disappointment; but a later message arrived to say that the Worcesters, coming from the 5th Brigade, would arrive that afternoon and relieve both of our battalions, who by that time were reduced to 540 Bedfords and 220 Cheshires altogether (the Bedfords having started with 1100 and the Cheshires with 600 odd).

In the evening a battalion of Worcesters —from goodness knows where—turned up and announced that they were to relieve us. We had already, as above mentioned, heard that they were coming, and were ready for them; but it was funny that they should arrive for only twenty-four hours, for the French were going to occupy our trenches on the morrow.

Anyhow, by midnight or so the Bedfords and Cheshires had cleared out, thankful to leave the horrible rabbit-warren where they had been stuck for nearly three wet, cold, and beastly weeks; and they retired to the wood and dug-outs close behind our château, so as to be in reserve in case of necessity.

Nov. 20th.

But they were not wanted as such, and the following day was fairly quiet as far as trench fighting was concerned.

But not so for the staff. We were sitting in the housekeeper's room after breakfast working out our orders for the withdrawal that night, when there was a terrific bang just outside the château—nearer than ever before. We looked at each other, and would, I verily believe, have settled down again to our work, so accustomed were we to shells of all sorts, had not Naylor, who had joined us two days before as temporary signal officer (*vice* Cadell, gone sick with light typhoid at Hille eighteen days before), jumped up and run outside in order to see where it had gone. Being Divisional signal officer, he had not, perhaps, had quite so much experience of shells as we had, and he wanted to get into closer touch. The example was infectious, and we also strolled out to see where the shell had fallen. Hardly had we got outside into the passage, and half-way up the basement steps into the fresh air, when there was a roar and an appalling crash which shook the building. The concussion made me stagger, and blew my cap off. St André's hat fizzed away into the bushes, and, surrounded by a cloud of red dust and stones and chips of balustrades and hunks of wood and branches, we held on to anything we could. No damage to ourselves; but a glance down the passage showed us that the shell, or most of it, had exploded in or just outside the kitchen, and blown that chamber, as well as the housekeeper's room, which we had just left, into absolute smithereens.

No time to look into further details; a hurried issue of orders, and we legged it for all we were worth across the open and into our funk-hole in the shrubbery 300 yards off, whilst the signal section and servants and orderlies made a bolt for the stables in the opposite direction.

But the Germans seem to have been satisfied with this little exhibition of "hate,"

and bombarded us no more—except casu-
ally, with shrapnel, as usual.   We crept
back to the château at intervals during the
morning, and removed various possessions
and chairs and tables to our dug-out, which
was not a very luxurious abode, though dry
and fairly deep.   Poor Conway, Weatherby's
servant, whom he had left behind, was the
only casualty; his dead body was found,
with both legs broken and an arm off, blown
down a cellar passage at the back.   The
next most serious casualty was Moulton-
Barrett's new pair of breeches, arrived that
morning from England, and driven full of
holes like a sugar-sifter.   Our late room
was a mass of wreckage—half the outer
wall and most of the inner one blown down,
tables and chairs and things overturned and
broken, and the floor knee-deep in plaster
and rubbish.   Of the kitchen there was still
less; and nothing was to be rescued from
the débris except one tin plate and one tin
mustard-pot.   It would have taken days to
clear it, for a good deal of the room above
seemed to have fallen into it as well, and
one could hardly get in at the door, so full
was the place of plaster, wreckage, and
stones, and hot-water pipes and bits of iron

and twisted rails, and dust and earth and broken laths and rafters. Luckily the concussion put the fire out, or there might have been still more damage.

We spent our day somewhat uncomfortably in the dug-out, for there was a hard frost and very little room to turn round in, and though we had a brazier, its charcoal fumes in the confined space nearly poisoned us. In the middle of the day three French officers turned up, and we made mutual arrangements for the taking over by them of this portion of the line, Milling (of the Bedfords) guiding one party and St André the other.

Food was rather a difficulty, for the mess servants had disappeared, and had last been seen hastening in the direction of Ypres— for which we cursed them loud and long. We did our best with small hunks of bully and odd bits of chocolate and a modicum of tea and biscuits in our haversacks—for all the rest of our food had been buried by that infernal shell,—but it was neither comfortable nor filling; and, in truth, as the dark winter evening came on with only one or two candle-stumps between us, we were not as happy as we should otherwise have been.

Help was, however, at hand; for our servants, Inskip and Stairs, who we thought had ignominiously run away, suddenly turned up with heaps of food. They had gone all the way to our cook's waggon three miles the other side of Ypres for comestibles, and whilst we were d—ing their eyes for bolting, were trudging, heavily laden, along the road back to us—good youths.

It was a lengthy business getting the relief through. The French troops, due at 7.30 P.M., did not arrive till 9.15 P.M., and even then it was difficult to pilot a lot of troops, fresh to the ground, in pitch darkness, over shell-holes and wires and broken trees and stumps, and through mud and undergrowth and dead horses, &c., &c., into the trenches destined for them. The details had to be very carefully arranged indeed, and it was not till nearly 2 A.M. that we had got the French into the trenches, the Worcesters into reserve, and the Bedfords and Cheshires on their way back to Ypres.

Then, with a sigh of some thankfulness apiece, we stumbled back in the darkness to the château, where we waited to collect the remains of the Signal Section and staff, and then moved off, mounted this time, down the Menin-Ypres road.

It was freezing very hard—as I think I remarked before—and the road was frightfully slippery. Trotting was almost out of the question, but I tried it on Squeaky for a few yards, on a dry broken bit. She pulled back on to the slippery part, slid up, and sat down heavily, whilst I fell gracefully off on to my shoulder. And she repeated the performance the other side of the town. Ypres, in the bright starlight, was still quite impressive, and the Cloth Hall was still almost intact. But there were many shell-holes about, and some of the houses were still smouldering. The town happened to be respited from shells for the actual moment, but I believe that the very next day a heavy bombardment began again, and the Cloth Hall was destroyed till hardly the skeleton thereof was left.

Nov. 21st.

We were due to billet in Locre, and there we arrived at about 7 A.M. It was frightfully cold, but, after we had seen the two battalions billeted, the military policeman who had been told to turn up and show us to our billets was nowhere to be found, so we wandered on as far as the Convent, staggering and slipping on the snowy ice and blowing on our fingers as we went. The thermometer must have shown ten degrees of frost or more, but I only know that I was very glad to reach our little house at last (having passed it already once half a mile before) and get in between the sheets of an ancient but respectably clean bed, covered by all the mackintoshes, blankets, and rugs I could get hold of.

The Cheshires were billeted on the Mont Rouge close by, and the Bedfords near us, at the corner of the Westoutre road. They had all struggled over the fourteen miles or so that divided them from their trenches, but having arrived and their feet having swollen terribly during the long march, any number of them could not get their boots on again, and they went to hospital by twenties and thirties, hobbling along the road with their feet tied up in rags or socks, for they were deformed with rheumatism and swollen joints,[1] and would not fit any boot. The Cheshires, as I expected, were much the worse of the two battalions, for

---

[1] What would now be known as "trench feet."

their trenches had been very wet, and most
of the men had sat with cold feet in water
for many days; yet there was not a single
case of pulmonary complaint amongst them,
and hardly even a cough or a cold.

Here we stayed, at Locre, till the 25th, the
men enjoying a most well-earned rest, and filling up with hot baths, warm clothes, socks,
parcels from home, and comforts of all sorts.
The Divisional Headquarters were in the
Convent, a clean huge building which did
very well for the purpose, and here we went
almost daily, either on business or on a meal
intent. The Cheshires—only 230 of them
left—were of no practical value, alas, with
their bad feet; so they were sent in to 2nd
Corps Headquarters (Sir H. S.-D.) at Bailleul,
nominally to "find" the Headquarters Guard,
but in reality to convalesce.

On the 25th we—that is, Headquarters and
the Bedfords, for that was all there was left
of the 15th for the moment—moved to St
Jan's Cappel, a nice little village only a few
miles behind Locre. We lived in the Curé's
(M. de Vos) house, clean and pleasant; and
the Curé, who liked the good things of this
world, brought his stout person to coffee
every evening, and did not disdain to make

the acquaintance of an occasional tot of British rum or whisky, except on Fridays.

Two days afterwards we were inspected both by Sir Horace and, half an hour later, by Sir John French, who were both pleased to say complimentary things of the Brigade. It did us good. The Bedfords again put me to confusion by calling out "'Ear! 'ear!" at telling points of the speeches—curious folk,—the only battalion I ever heard do so. 587 men and 8 officers on parade, not one of the latter of whom, except the Quartermaster, had come out with the battalion. Griffith was on leave, his place being taken by Major Mackenzie, V.C., who had just joined. All the other officers who had left Ireland with me in August were either killed, wounded, or sick.

We were under orders to go into the trenches again shortly, taking over from Maude,[1] now commanding the 14th Brigade; he also had the Dorsets and Norfolks, scraped up from various places, attached to him. His line was in front of Dranoutre.

On the 29th November we took over there, a most complicated arrangement which only evolved itself clearly during the next week.

[1] The victor of Baghdad.

I had the East Surreys and Manchesters
under me for a time, and then the K.O.S.B.'s,
all interchanging and intershuffling with my
battalions, the main reason being that I had
not got the Cheshires, so had to shift as best
I could without them, picking up a battalion
of the 13th or 14th Brigade when one was
available.

The line was not exactly nice. We had,
it is true, got rid of the worst bit, Hill 73, on
to the 3rd Division, which was next door on
the left; but it extended all the same for an
unpleasant length on our right, which was
south of the Wulverghem - Messines road,
the right of the Brigade on our right being
on the Douve. At the longest—the length
that the Brigade had to defend varied
according to circumstances — the line was
just over 2500 yards; at its shortest it was
about 2200. Considering that the normal
frontage (defensive) of the Brigade at full
strength was 900 to 1300 yards, this was a
bit "thin" in more senses than one.

As we were here for three months, off and
on—from the beginning of December to the
end of February,—it may be worth while
trying to describe it, if I can.

Imagine a bit of rolling country—rather

like parts of Leicestershire,—fair-sized fields, separated mostly by straggling fences interspersed with wire (largely barbed), and punctuated by tall trees. Patches of wood in places, spinney size for the most part. Low hills here and there—Kemmel, Scherpenberg, Ploegsteert Wood,—but all outside our area. For villages, Dranoutre, Neuve Eglise, Wulverghem, and Lindenhoek, of which the two last were already more than half shot to pieces and almost deserted. Opposite our right was Messines—a mile and a half in front of our line,—its big, square, old church tower still standing; it may have had a spire on the top, but if so it had disappeared before we came. Nearly opposite our extreme left, but out of our jurisdiction and in the sphere of the Division on our left, was Wytschaete (pronounce Wich Khâte), one and a half miles off. The cavalry had held both Messines [1] and Wytschaete at the end of October, but had been overwhelmingly attacked here and driven out of them, so that the two villages formed a hostile bulge into our line. We had been in hopes of driving attacks into the base of the bulge and thus forcing a retirement. But the

[1] Locally pronounced Mersé.

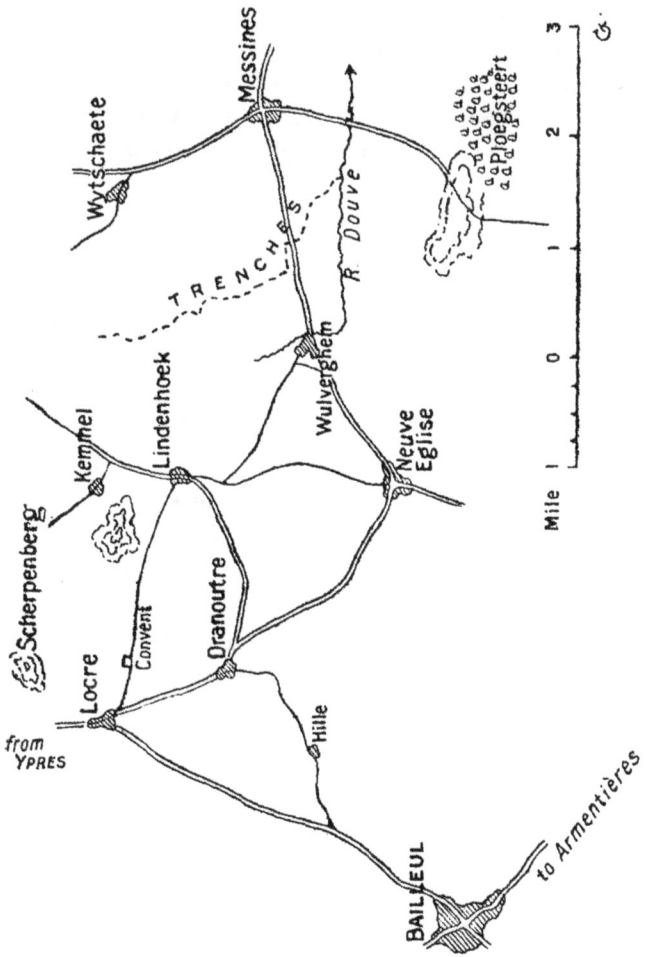

Germans reinforced the bulge and entrenched it heavily, and instead of our cutting off the bulge, it became flatter and flatter, without giving way at the point, so that we had to retire slightly, on either side, and not they.

Farms, nearly all of them roofless and half - ruined, were dotted about over the country. Small ones for the most part they were, and of the usual type—a liquid and stinking manure-heap surrounded on three sides by a living-house and barns. Of the roads, those from Dranoutre to Lindenhoek, Dranoutre to Neuve Eglise, and Neuve Eglise *viâ* Wulverghem to Messines, were *pavé* — *i.e.*, cobble-stones down the centre and mud on both sides. Those joining Lindenhoek to Neuve Eglise and Wulverghem were also mostly *pavé*. The remainder were mere field tracks for the most part, rarely metalled, and in wet weather almost impassable for mud.

O that mud! We have heard lots about Flanders mud, but the reality transcends imagination, especially in winter. Greasy, slippery, holding clay, over your toes in most places and over your ankles in all the rest—where it is not over your knees,—it is the most horrible "going" I know anywhere. Whether you are moving across plough or grass fields, or along lanes, you are perpetually skating about and slipping up on the firmer bits and held fast by the ankles in the softer ones. There is no stone in the district, nothing but rich loamy clay, *alias* mud. However much you dig, you never come across stone, nothing but sticky mud which clings to your shovel and refuses to be parted from it—mud that has to be scraped off at almost every stroke, mud that absorbs water like a sponge yet refuses to give it up again. Every little puddle and rut, every hoof-depression full of rain, remains like that for weeks; even when the weather is fine the water does not seem to evaporate, but remains on the surface.

And when it rains, as it did all that winter (except when it snowed), the state of the trenches is indescribable. Some were, frankly, so full of water that they had to be abandoned, and a breastwork erected behind. But a breastwork is slow work, especially if you are less than 100 yards from the enemy. For weeks, indeed, the garrison of one particular trench had to lie out on the mud, or on what waterproofs

R

they could get, behind a shelter two to three feet high—always growing a little, yet never to be made to a real six feet height for reason of conspicuousness and consequent clusters of Black Marias.

Other trenches varied from five inches to five feet deep in mud; in one a Dorset man was literally almost drowned and drawn forth with great difficulty. Many cases occurred of semi-submersion, and as for moving up the communication trenches during the winter, it was generally an impossibility, for they were either knee-deep in water or in mud, and simply refused to be drained. So men preferred the risk of a stray bullet to the certainty of liquid mud to the knees and consequent icy discomfort for twenty-four hours and more. And as for the unfortunate ration-parties and men bringing up heavy trench stores, their task was really one of frightful labour, for, for two men to cross a large and slippery muddy series of fields carrying a 100 lb. box between them was no joke. First one would slide up and skate off in one direction whilst the other did his best to hold on, generally resulting in dropping his end of the box or finding himself on the flat of his back. Then the parts would be reversed, but they always slid up in opposite directions — the mud saw to that,—and they would arrive in the trenches, after their stroll of a mile or less, absolutely exhausted and dripping with sweat. It was difficult enough, over much of the ground, to avoid slipping up even when burdened by nothing more than a walking-stick; that I know from personal experience. Yet for many weeks the men had to do this and suffer, for fascines and bricks, besides sandbags, were only just beginning to make their appearance in December; and floor-boards and gratings and gravel and trench stores and wire-netting, and revetments and planks and iron sheeting and trestles and hurdles of all sorts, did not really materialize in anything like sufficient numbers till March.

The draining of the trenches was heartbreaking. After a heavy day or two of rain the parapets would fall down in hunks into the foot of water or so in the trenches, and would churn up into liquid mud, only to be removed by large spoons, of which we had none, or buckets, of which we had but very few. It was too thick to drain off down the very, very gradual slopes which

were the best we could do, and too liquid
to be shovelled away; so there it would
remain, and our strenuous efforts in re-
building the parapets (for at this period
we had no revetting material) would only
result, a night or two later, in still further
collapses.

The R.E. companies, both 17th and 59th,
worked like heroes, and so particularly did
the Norfolks and Bedfords; but it was
most disheartening work. No sooner was
one parapet fairly complete than another
fell in; and when this was mended the
first one would collapse again under the
incessant downpour. And all this time wire
entanglements had to be put up in front
under hostile fire, trenches connected up
and drained, support trenches dug, communication trenches improved, loopholes
made, defences thickened and strengthened,
saps pushed out, all under the fire of an
enemy anything from 60 to 200 yards off,
and always on rather higher ground than
ourselves, worse luck, so that he had the
whip-hand.

Soon came the period of hand grenades,
in which he had six to one the best of us
in numbers; and then in rifle grenades

ditto ditto; and then in trench mortars, flare - lights, searchlights, and rockets — wherein we followed him feebly and at a great distance; for where he sent up 100 (say) light balls at night, we could only afford five or six; and other things in proportion. Later on came the Minenwerfer, an expanded type of trench mortar, and its bomb, but up to the end of February his efforts in this direction were not very serious, though I allow that he did us more harm thereby than we him. For our trench mortars were in an experimental stage, made locally by the R.E., and constructed of thin gas-pipe iron and home-made jam-pot bombs, whose behaviour was always erratic, and sometimes, I regret to say, fatal to the mortarist. (Poor Rogers, R.E., a capital subaltern, was killed thus, besides others, I fear.)

Our reliefs varied. Normally the Brigade was supposed to be, at first, eight days in and four days out. Then this was rapidly changed to twelve days in and six days out; then, as the 14th Brigade suggested that it should hold Neuve Eglise, a quite short front, in perpetuity, whilst the 13th and 15th Brigades relieved each other alternate

eight days along the long front, it was
changed nominally to eight in and eight
out. But it was not always possible, and
our last tour lasted twenty days in and
only three out.

The reliefs made one's head whirl. It
was all right to start with, two battalions
in the trenches (*i.e.*, fire-trenches, support-
trenches, and reserve-trenches), and two
battalions in reserve at Dranoutre or thereabouts — four days about, each battalion,
in eight-day reliefs, or three days about in
twelve-day reliefs. This was simple. But
when our line was lengthened to a three-
battalion length it became much more difficult, especially when one battalion was much
weaker than the other three. And when,
eventually, the brigade was presented with
a Territorial battalion of great strength but
no experience, making five battalions of vary-
ing strengths to occupy a three-battalion
length, whilst one could only put the Territorial one (at first) into a comparatively safe
place in the line which did not fit it, then
the problem of the wolf, the goat, and the
cabbage faded into complete insignificance.

It was very difficult to fit everything in so
that each battalion had its fair share of duty

and of rest. Even with the best intentions matters did not always pan out straight, for considerations of strength, of comparative excellence, of dangerous and of safe localities, of moral, of comfortable or uncomfortable trenches, of spade-work and of a dozen other things, had to be fitted together like a Chinese puzzle.

There was a particularly dangerous and uncomfortable length which was given to the best battalion to hold. On its relief, who should hold it? the next best, who was badly wanted somewhere else, or another one weak in numbers and consequently unfit? And when the relief came again, was the best battalion always to be doomed to the worst and most dangerous trenches, merely because it *was* the best? Hardly an incitement to good work. And when the battalions did not fit their length, were you to add or subtract a company from somebody else, or would you put some in reserve out of their turn, thereby inflicting unfair hardship on another battalion? And would you like to reinforce one battalion, in case of attack, by another battalion? or would you like to make it thin in front and deep behind, and support itself? If the other thing was necessary, how could you do it when the two battalions were accustomed to relieve their companies, internally, in different ways, when perhaps the transport of one was deficient, or one battalion preferred sandbags, whilst the other cherished hurdles, as revetting material?—for I always found that giving the commanding officer his head in such small internal matters produced the best work. It was a matter for deep study and wet towels, and there let it rest.

We had much difficulty about quarters outside the trenches, for all the farmhouses anywhere within two miles of the enemy were shelled pretty regularly as regards quantity of explosive material devoted to them—though, as regards dates, they varied considerably. Battalion headquarters had to be dumped down in farms half shot to pieces, with all windows broken and howling icy draughts tearing through the shell-holed walls. If you did not like this, you could go and dig a big hole in the side of a road or a turnip-field and live in that. The reserves were always the difficulty, and so, for a long time, were even the supports. For whatever and wherever the trenches that we dug for them, the rain came steadily down and broke away the sides of the dug-outs and provided wet legs for those that sat therein. Later on, more timber being available, as well as iron sheeting, hurdles and other things, they became a good deal more weather-proof; but at first the men as well as the officers were, I fear, very uncomfortable.

In those days one could not dream of going up to or into a trench except in the dark, or, indeed, of moving about anywhere near there except at night. Nowadays one can visit all one's trenches in broad daylight, and never care a rap for the occasional bullets which whistle over the comfortable deep communication trenches; but up to the spring of 1915 it was very different almost throughout.

I used to visit the trenches every third night or so; at least I tried to, but it was not by any means always possible. It meant a three-mile ride there, putting up the horses in Wulverghem or Lindenhoek, and a walk of a mile or so to the trenches, then a mile or less along the trenches. It was lucky for you if there was any light of moon or stars to see by, and lucky if you did not go over your knees in mud in the dark. On one occasion it came down a pitchy dead blackness just as I was arriving at the trenches, so that you literally could not see your hand in front, or the road, or anything else; so I gave it up and went back. Other nights were impossible for the same reason; and occasionally the brilliance of the moon was in fault, though not often. So we had to select our nights carefully.

Johnston, V.C.,[1] R.E., was in R.E. charge of our trenches. (Poor fellow, he was killed by a sniper near St Eloi on April 15.) He must have worked something like eighteen hours out of the twenty-four. For by 9 A.M. he was collecting material near Dranoutre and receiving reports, and settling his company administrative work. At 11.30 he came to see me, and we discussed and settled the ensuing night's task. Then back to his farm to give out instructions to his sappers, and fifty other things to do before he rode out about 6 P.M. to the trenches, remaining there till 3 A.M. or even 6 A.M. — to superintend the work and struggle about in the mud all night. He never

[1] He had received the V.C. for a particularly plucky piece of raft work under heavy fire at Missy.

spared himself an ounce. He was occasionally so nearly dead with want of sleep that I once or twice ordered him to take a night's sleep; but he always got out of it on some pretext or other.

And with it all he was as plucky as the devil — he seemed to like getting shot at. One night he got a ricochet bullet over his heart, but this only put him in a furious rage (if you can use the word about such a seeming mild person), and spent the next twenty-four hours in collecting ammunition and bombs and extra trench-mortars and firing them himself; this seemed to soothe him. He was a wonderful fellow all round, always full of expedients and never disheartened by the cruel collapse of all his plans caused by the wet weather; and if there was a dangerous piece of work on hand, he was always first in giving the lead. One very nasty place on the left there was which was commanded by the enemy at short range, yet we could not dig in it, as the water was only a foot below the ground, and breastworks there were practically impossible; yet if the enemy had seized this bit they would have enfiladed the rest of the line; why they did not do so I do not know.   He was always pressing me to attack the Germans at this point and seize a bit of false crest that they held; but my better judgment was against it, as, if we had taken the bit, we should have been commanded there from three sides instead of one, and could not have held it for half an hour.   I know Johnston's private opinion of me in this matter was that I was a funk, but he was too polite to say so.   After I left, the following Brigade not only did not attack the point, but fell back some distance here, "on its own"; and I am sure they were right.

Poor Johnston—he became Brigade-Major after Weatherby left for the 5th Divisional Staff (some time in April 1915, I think), and, as I remarked, was killed shortly afterwards. His death was a very heavy loss to the Brigade.

At Dranoutre we—that is, the Brigade staff—lived in a perpetual atmosphere of mud and draughts.   The Curé's house was very small and very dirty, and was not improved by the pounds of mud which every one brought in on his boots at all hours of the day and left on our best drugget—a cheap, thin thing which I bought in Bailleul (they had not such a thing as a carpet in the whole town) wherewith to cover the nakedness of the brick floor of the one tiny room in which we all worked and ate.

Weatherby and I slept in the house, and the others were billeted outside, but the quarters were none of them more than passable — poor villagers' rooms, with a frowzy though comfortable bed, a rickety washhand-stand, if you were lucky (I did not even have that), no carpet on the dirty wooden floor, and one small hard-backed chair, generally minus a portion of a leg; never any chest of drawers or anywhere to put your things, as if there by any chance was such a thing in the room, it was sure to be full of the inhabitants' rusty old black clothes and dirty blue flannel shirts, and petticoats, thick and musty, by the ton,—I never saw so many petticoats per inhabitant.

Our mess had only had one change since the beginning of the war, and that was in the signal officer. Cadell had gone sick in November, and Miles had replaced him in December. For about a month, including all the period at Ypres, we had had no signal officer (except Naylor for two days),

nor any Brigade-Major from about the
12th November (at Ypres) till the beginning
of December; so Sergeant King, a first-rate
signaller, though not the senior, had carried
on for Cadell, and Moulton-Barrett had
added the duties of Brigade-Major to his
own.   But by the middle of December we
were complete again.   Weatherby had returned from his sick leave, and Miles, of
the K.O.S.B.'s, was now signalling officer.
A quite excellent one he was, too — very
silent, always an hour or two late for
dinner (owing to strenuous night work),
never asking questions, but always doing
things before they were even suggested,
and very thoroughly at that; he was a
great acquisition.   Moulton-Barrett was
still Staff Captain—very hard-working and
conscientious, and very thorough; Weatherby was still Brigade-Major—keen and resourceful; Beilby was still veterinary officer
—capable and helpful; and St André was
still interpreter and billeting officer—cheer-
ful and most willing.   His duties were
mostly to investigate the numerous cases
of natives who wanted to go somewhere
or do something—generally to fetch their
cows off a shell-swept field, or to rescue

their furniture from a burnt village, or to fetch or buy something from Bailleul—and recommend them (or otherwise) to me for passes—a most trying duty, wearing to the temper; but he was angelic in patience, and, as a light recreation, used to accompany me to the trenches fairly often.

One case there was where, for three nights running, great fids of wire were cut out of some artillery cables connecting them with their observers—a most reprehensible deed. So I had patrols out to spy along the lines,—no result, except that next morning another 100 yards had gone. So I made St André publish a blood-and-thunder proclamation threatening death to any one found tampering with our wires. Spies were plentiful, and a gap in our wires might be fatal.

And then the culprit owned up. It was an old woman near whose cottage the wires passed, and her fences required mending.

Neuve Eglise, which we inhabited for a fortnight or more, and where we spent Xmas Day, was a good cut above Dranoutre. Except for the first three days, when we lived with a doctor,—and his stove smoked frightfully till we discovered a dead starling in the pipe,—we dwelt in exceeding comfort, comparatively speaking. It was a brewer's house, about the biggest in the village—which was three times the size of Dranoutre, — with real furniture in it, a real dining-room (horribly cold, as the stove refused to work), and a most comfortable series of highly civilized bedrooms. (Last time I was in the neighbourhood—August 1915—there was long grass in the streets, not a soul in the place, half the houses in absolute ruins, and our late quarters with one side missing and three parts of the house as well.) The trenches were much less pestered with shells and bullets than the Dranoutre lot, and it was easier work altogether for the men. We quite enjoyed it, and on Xmas Day so did the Germans. For they came out of their trenches and walked across unarmed, with boxes of cigars and seasonable remarks. What were our men to do? Shoot? You could not shoot unarmed men. Let them come? You could not let them come into your trenches; so the only thing feasible at the moment was done—and some of our men met them half-way and began talking to them.

We got into trouble for doing it. But, after all, it is difficult to see what we could otherwise have done, unless we shot the very first unarmed man who showed himself — *pour encourager les autres;* but we did not know what he was going to do. Meanwhile our officers got excellent close views of the German trenches, and we profited accordingly; the Boche did not, for he was not allowed close enough to ours.

Which reminds me that on one occasion, when going round the trenches, I asked a man whether he had had any shots at the Germans. He responded that there was an elderly gentleman with a bald head and a long beard who often showed himself over the parapet.

"Well, why didn't you shoot him?"

"Shoot him?" said the man; "why, Lor' bless you, sir, 'e's never done *me* no 'arm!" A case of "live and let live," which is certainly not to be encouraged. But cold-blooded murder is never popular with our men.

Talking of anecdotes, and the trend of our men's minds, I heard that on another occasion a groom, an otherwise excellent creature, wrote home to his "girl" thus: "Me and the master rode out to the

s

trenches last night.   We was attacked by
a strong German patrol.   I nips off me
horse, pulls out my rifle and shoots two
of them, and the rest bolted."   Not a single
atom of truth in the story, except that
he was nestling in a warm stable at an
advanced village, whilst his master was
shivering in the mud of the trenches that
night.

Another gem was a statement by a Transport officer's servant that he had shot 1200
Germans himself with a machine-gun.   This
was a man who, I verily believe, had never
even been within earshot of a gun, much
less seen a German, his duties being ex-
clusively several miles in rear of the firing
line.   And, being a civilian up till quite
recently, I am sure he did not know the
muzzle of a maxim from its breech.

During our tours in "Divisional reserve"
we generally spent the time in St Jan's
Cappel (already described) or Bailleul.   The
latter town, with its rather quaint old brick
fourteenth - century church, porched à la
Louis Quinze, was tolerable rather than
admirable.   Nothing of civil interest, and
hardly anything to buy except magnificent
grapes from the "Grapperies," even in

November. We housed a battalion or more in the man's series of greenhouses, and he responded — after several more battalions had been quartered there—with a claim for 2,000,000 francs. He could not prove that a single pane of glass or any of his vines had been broken, nor any grapes stolen, for indeed they had not been, but he based his claim on the damage done to them by tobacco smoke (which I always thought was particularly good for them), and by the report of the big guns, which shattered the vines' nerves so that he was sure they would not produce again (also a fallacy, for I had some more excellent grapes there nearly a year afterwards—September '15). I did not hear what compensation he got, but he would have been lucky to get 20 francs.

I once went into a poorly furnished watch-maker's shop, but the lady there could do nothing for my watch. She told me that, being an optician in a small way as well, she had had a whole stock of spectacles and glasses. When the Germans came through the town in October, they demanded field-glasses. The few ones she had they stole, and then because she had no more they stole her watchmaker's tools, and swept all the spectacles and glasses and watches on to the floor and stamped them to powder.

There is really little more to relate about our time at Dranoutre and neighbourhood. It was a time of a certain amount of nerve-strain, for we all knew that our trenches were by no means perfect, and that if the enemy did attack us we should have great difficulty in bringing up reserves in time to beat them off; for we could not keep them under cover within decent range—there were no billets or houses,—and if we dug trenches for them they were not only exposed to the enemy's shell fire but were certain to be half full of water in two days; whilst we could not get anything like enough trench stores and timber, and what we did get we had enormous difficulty in bringing up to the trenches.

During all this time the artillery helped us all they knew, and were extremely well run, first by Ballard, then Saunders, and then Sandys, as Brigade Commanders. But they were badly handicapped by want of shells, especially howitzer high explosives, and we had to suffer a great deal of shell fire without returning it.

We used to average about four casualties

a day in each battalion, say fifteen to twenty a day in the Brigade, which made a big hole in the strengths. Officers were always getting killed—often, alas, their own fault, through excess of zeal; and men used perpetually to lose their lives through getting out of the trenches in order to stretch their half-frozen limbs. Sickness was, strange to say, almost negligible. There were far more cases of arthritis and other things due to cold wet feet than anything else; and the men were extraordinarily healthy, comparatively speaking, considering the desperately uncomfortable hard life.

General Morland was, of course, commanding the Division during this time, and used to come nearly every morning in his car to see us; also Sir C. Fergusson, now Corps Commander, often came.

But during the whole of that winter there was very little for the higher commands to do, except to collect and send up material for the trenches, and to try and keep pace with the German developments — for we could do little or nothing in the way of offensive action.

I tried to get the thing neatly organised, as to stores and times and amounts and transport for taking the things up to the trenches; but it was very difficult, as sometimes there were no engineer stores to be had, or the wires got broken by shell fire and took a long time to repair, or it was more urgent to bring up rations or water or ammunition, and the requisite transport for all was not available. But all the same, the trenches gradually improved.

At last, on the 18th February, we got news that there was to be a move from our present line. The fact was that the 28th Division (also the 27th), composed of white troops from India and other tropical places, had had an exceedingly nasty time. Many of the men were rotten with fever, and the cold wet weather had sent scores and scores into hospital. They had been put into the trenches round St Eloi to relieve the French, who had held all the line round here chiefly with their field artillery and a very few men; and the trenches were, consequently, most sketchy, according to British ideas, and the approaches under heavy fire. The French did not mind, for, if they were shelled out of their trenches, as often happened, they just skipped out of them and turned their guns on till the Germans were cleared out; and then they went back again. But this sort of thing did not suit us; and when the Germans did attack our trenches here they took a good many and we lost a lot of men, especially when we tried to counter-attack and retake them. So the 28th Division was *hors de combat* for the moment, and was sent down to recuperate in a quieter area — which was that of the 5th Division.

Our orders were for the 13th and 15th Brigades to move north to St Eloi and be replaced by the 83rd and 84th Brigades. This was done,—a most complicated move, for the 84th Brigade, which fell to our lot, was composed of four very weak battalions, and we had five battalions, mostly rather strong; and by the 24th February we had six battalions, including the 9th Londons (an excellent battalion) and 6th Cheshires (a strong and hard-working one).

We ought to have been relieved, in the normal state of affairs, on the 17th February, but we were kept on, as a matter of fact, till the 27th, because of this new arrangement.

On that morning I received word that

an extraordinary lamp message had been
read during the night in the enemy's lines
by a signaller of the 6th Cheshires. It
was a long, confused message in English,
repeating that "the hill" was going to be
attacked at noon on that day, with messages about "B.C. codes"—whatever that
may be,—trumpery wire entanglements, the
unready English, good leading essential, &c.,
and a lot of other undecipherable nonsense.
The whole message had lasted nearly two
hours, with interruptions and repetitions.
I did not know what to make of it. It
was probably a "leg-pull," or somebody
practising his English; but as there was
a 1000 to 1 chance of its being sent by
some sympathiser in our front, and of
the projected "attack" being a real one,
I sent two companies down as a reserve
to the Bus Farm in our reserve line, and
held a battery ready before its time. But
nothing happened, and we were relieved
without incident.

Bols, by the way, had, from commanding
the Dorsets, been appointed to command
the 84th Brigade, and he took over before
leaving, on the day before we left. I was
very sorry indeed to lose him, but knew

that, once his foot was well on the ladder, he would go right ahead—as he has.[1] The same applied to Ballard, who also had been given a Brigade—the 7th.

The 15th Brigade thereupon retired into billets at Bailleul, with orders to stay there for three days only, and then to go straight to St Eloi and take over these trenches of the 28th Division. Not much rest—twenty days in the trenches, three out, and then trenches again.

As regards myself, however, my days of connection with the Brigade were numbered. I had heard, with mixed but pleasant feelings, that I had been promoted Major-General "for distinguished service" on the 18th February (Weatherby got a brevet majority in the same 'Gazette'), and I was now ordered to go home and report myself in London. My successor was to be Northey, of the 60th Rifles, from Givenchy way, and he turned up on the 2nd March at our Headquarters, which were then at 28 Rue de Lille. I at once recognised that he would carry on excellently well, and had no compunction in leaving the command in his hands. All

[1] He is now (1917) Major-General.

that was left for me to do was to take
a tender farewell of the officers of the
Brigade and of my staff, and to publish a
final farewell order to the old Brigade.   I
was very sad at leaving, and had I known
what an awful time they were going to
have at St Eloi and Hill 60, I should have
been sadder still.[1]   Of all the regimental
officers and men who had left Ireland with
me on the 14th August 1914, six and a half
months previously, I could count on my
ten fingers the number of officers left :—

Norfolks—Done[2] and Bruce (both ill in
    hospital   from   strenuous   overwork),
    Megaw (killed later), Paterson.
Dorsets—Ransome, Partridge.
Bedfords — Griffith[2] (trustiest of C.O.'s,
    who had been under heavier fire than
    almost any one in the Brigade, yet never
    touched), Allason (thrice wounded), Gled-
    stanes (killed later).
Cheshires—Frost (killed later).

I do not think there was another officer
except the quartermasters — Smith (Nor-

---

[1] They lost 2400 men out of not quite 4000 in a fortnight
in April.
[2] Now (1917) commanding a Brigade.

folks), Sproule (Cheshires), and Pearce (Bed-fords)[1]; and as for the men, there may have been ten or so per battalion, but I really do not think there were more.

I took the evening train at Bailleul and spent an agreeable evening with Ker Seymer, the train officer. I got to Boulogne and on board the boat at midnight, and next day, the 3rd March, saw me arrive at 8.30 A.M. in London.

[1] The Dorset one had been promoted.

.

www.ingramcontent.com/pod-product-compliance
Lightning Source LLC
Chambersburg PA
CBHW030408100426
42812CB00028B/2871/J